the OREGON FARM TABLE COOKBOOK

the OREGON FARM TABLE COOKBOOK

101 Homegrown Recipes from the Pacific Wonderland

KARISTA BENNETT

The Countryman Press
A Division of W. W. Norton & Company
Independent Publishers Since 1923

For information about special discounts for bulk purchases, please contact
W. W. Norton Special Sales at specialsales@wwnorton.com or 800-233-4830

Manufacturing by Versa Press
Production manager: Gwen Cullen

The Countryman Press
www.countrymanpress.com

A division of W. W. Norton & Company, Inc.
500 Fifth Avenue, New York, NY 10110
www.wwnorton.com

978-1-68268-500-6 (pbk.)

10 9 8 7 6 5 4 3 2 1

For Craig, Alexandria, and Amelia—you are the food for my soul

Each season is like a little treasure box filled with the gift of food.

CONTENTS

Entrées

Desserts

Dressings, Condiments, Salsas, and Sauces

INTRODUCTION

In 2002, my family and I moved to the enchanting Pacific Northwest. After living in Washington State for several years, we are now proud to call Oregon home. However, it wasn't until setting out to research this book that I truly came to know it. Oregon is a diverse landscape of rugged shoreline dotted with fishing communities, densely pined mountain ranges with sprawling ranches, lush valleys with rich soil, and high desert plains that extend beyond the sunrise. Its terrain is visually inspiring and home to some of the freshest, most delicious food and wine in the country.

While traveling the state, I had the privilege of meeting and mingling with remarkable individuals—makers, farmers, growers, and producers—who impacted my life in ways I never expected. I am immensely grateful for these earnest and hard-working people and, in some respects, I feel as if I've gained a new family of friends.

The Oregon Farm Table Cookbook tells the story of a handful of inspiring individuals who are devoted to producing clean, healthy, and sustainable food. These farmers, chefs, fishermen, food artisans, brewers, and wine makers are committed to providing the highest-quality food for their communities while nurturing our magical landscapes.

The state's farm-to-table movement has been steadfast for decades and is continuously supported by the Oregon State University Extension Service's Small Farms program, which is a national leader in applied research and education. Despite the ever-changing fads of subscription meal boxes and special diets, Oregon's small farms have continued to grow through support systems, bringing new generations of farmers and food producers into the fold.

Each food and drink producer is passionate in the belief that locally grown and sourced food is the most sustainable way to feed a community.

The compelling human stories told here are paired with beautiful images and approachable recipes created with fresh, seasonal ingredients. This book is filled with 101 recipes that result in a feast for the eyes, food for the soul, and a treasure for the kitchen.

It is my deepest hope that these stories and recipes will inspire you to gather with family, friends, and community, and to create food that is flavorful, healthful, and whole. I've always believed that food is the element that brings us to the table, where life is lived and memories are made.

With love and peace from my table to yours,

Karista

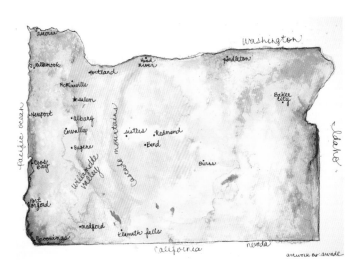

Map of Oregon State

COOKING TERMS

I am often asked specific cooking term–related questions such as "What is the difference between chopping and dicing?" or "Is panfrying the same thing as sautéing?" To make preparing these recipes easier, I've added a list of cooking terms with definitions that I use throughout the book.

I believe recipes are excellent tools for success in the kitchen. However, I also believe recipes are guidelines and not always the rule. I encourage you to use the recipes in this book and enjoy them, but I also advise tailoring them to you and your family's tastes. Have fun with the ingredients and don't be afraid to substitute with a more preferred ingredient.

Bake: To cook using dry heat, e.g., an oven.

Blanch: To cook an ingredient briefly in hot water before the finishing or final cooking process.

Braise: To sauté meat or vegetables, which are then slowly cooked over low heat.

Brown or pan sear: A cooking technique that browns the surface of food in fat over high heat before finishing by another method, such as braising or roasting, in order to add flavor.

Chop: To cut into pieces of approximately the same size.

Dice: To cut ingredients into cubes; a small dice is approximately ¼-inch squares, a medium dice is approximately ½-inch squares, and a large dice is approximately ¾-inch squares.

Emulsify: To slowly combine a fat (such as butter or oil) with another liquid (such as vinegar, lime juice, or water) to create a creamy, silky sauce.

Garnish: To add finishing touches to your prepared dish, such as fresh herbs, edible flowers, or fruit.

Mince: To cut ingredients into pieces smaller than ⅛-inch squares. This is typically used for pungent ingredients, such as garlic.

Panfry: This method uses much less oil than deep frying but more oil than a typical sauté.

Poach: To cook in simmering liquid that is 160°F to 185°F.

Puree: To mash, strain, or chop an ingredient, turning it into a smooth paste.

Reduce: To thicken a liquid and concentrate its flavor by boiling or simmering.

Roast: A dry-heat cooking method; to cook in an oven until golden brown, such as roasted vegetables and meats.

Roux: Typically flour and a fat (butter or fat from a meat protein) that cooks into a paste for the purpose of thickening soups and sauces.

Sauté: To cook ingredients quickly on the stovetop using a small amount of fat, such as olive oil or butter.

Simmer: To cook slowly on a stovetop while maintaining a temperature just below boiling. The temperature range for simmering is 185°F to 200°F.

Spoon-and-level method: To use a spoon to gently fill a measuring cup before leveling it off with the back of a knife or straight edge.

Wilt: A process that warms leafy greens to the point where they look wilted with a droopy appearance.

Zest: To gently scrape or shred pieces of the outer rind of citrus. The zest of any citrus contains intense oils that enhance the flavor of many recipes.

BREAKFAST AND BRUNCH

Lavender Cream Biscuits

MAKES SIX 3-INCH BISCUITS

There is nothing that makes my family happier than waking up to the scent of freshly baked biscuits on a Sunday morning. This recipe is simple to whip up and I can have them ready and on the breakfast table in 30 minutes. Instead of cutting in butter, I use a recipe that incorporates 1½ cups of heavy cream into the mix and creates the lightest, tastiest biscuit.

Lavender is abundant in Oregon and it makes the loveliest addition to all sorts of sweet and savory dishes. It is especially so in these biscuits. If you're out and about, Sweet Delilah Flower Farm on Sauvie Island is where you'll find not only fresh lavender, but other gorgeous seasonal blooms as well.

I've included the recipe for lavender sugar below, which I keep on hand for biscuits and other baked goods and savory recipes. Sometimes I even add a smidgen of this lavender sugar to my afternoon tea.

Lavender Sugar

1 cup granulated sugar

2 tablespoons dried culinary lavender

Biscuits

**2 cups all-purpose flour, using the spoon-
    and-level method**

2 tablespoons baking powder

½ teaspoon salt

2 tablespoons Lavender Sugar

1½ cups heavy cream, plus more as needed

2 tablespoons unsalted butter, melted

1. Preheat the oven to 425ºF.

2. To make the Lavender Sugar, add the sugar and dried culinary lavender to the bowl of a food processor. Mix the sugar and lavender for a minute or two, until the lavender is nicely infused into the sugar. You should see small specks of lavender throughout the sugar. Place the lavender sugar in a glass jar with a lid and store in a cool location for up to 1 month.

3. To make the biscuits, add flour, baking powder, salt, and 1 tablespoon Lavender Sugar to a medium bowl. Mix to combine. Stir in the heavy cream and mix until all the ingredients are nicely incorporated.

4. Transfer the biscuit dough to a floured surface and form a disc. Roll out the dough to about 1 inch in thickness and cut biscuits with a 3-inch biscuit cutter. Do not twist the biscuit cutter, simply press down and then pull up and pop out the biscuit onto a parchment paper–lined baking sheet.

5. Mix together the melted butter with remaining tablespoon Lavender Sugar and brush or spoon and smear over the top of each biscuit. This will form a lovely, sweet, and fragrant biscuit crust.

6. Place the biscuits in the oven and bake for about 15 minutes, or until the tops are golden brown. Remove the biscuits from the oven and let them cool slightly before serving.

SWEET DELILAH FLOWER FARM

CHELSEA WILLIS / SAUVIE ISLAND, OREGON

As I stepped onto the Sweet Delilah Flower Farm, I was greeted with the scent of fresh earth, spring flowers, and a plethora of herbs. Chelsea Willis, founder and farmer of Sweet Delilah Flower Farm, is an impressive young woman with a background in psychology. A graduate of the Floral Design Institute and Floret, she's also a counselor for youth and an ardent meditation practitioner and teacher who has a passion for human connection. She started Sweet Delilah Flower Farm as a way to bring people together and as a place of community and healing.

This enchanting flower farm is found on Sauvie Island along the Columbia River, just ten miles north of Portland. Sweet Delilah Flower Farm is home to a stunning selection of organically grown flowers. Chelsea provides these in the form of fresh bouquets, a U-pick option, farm-to-vase floral design, à la carte wedding services, and classes to the community. She also offers a variety of organically grown medicinal herbs, fresh and dried, to local herbalists and medicine makers.

Now Chelsea is expanding beyond the borders of Sauvie Island to bring fresh blooms directly to her customers. During the summer season, you'll find the Sweet Delilah Farm Flower Truck—the first of its kind—at various pop-up locations around Portland.

The mobile flower boutique is anything but a delivery truck. Chelsea describes it as the farm-to-vase, meet-your-grower, flower-happy hour, sunshine-and-goodness slinger that you'll want at your next special occasion or event. Most of all, she loves that it allows businesses to commune with the locals over flower petals and good vibes.

Marionberry Streusel Muffins

MAKES 12 TO 16 MUFFINS

Oregon has the perfect climate for growing an abundance of berries. Along with rich volcanic soil, cool spring months and a hot summer season help produce berries that are relished all year long.

The most popular berries to be found are strawberries, blueberries, raspberries, cherries, cranberries, and several varieties of blackberries. One particular variety of blackberry that is prized for its tart but sweet flavor is the marionberry. In 1956, they were grown in Marion County, Oregon, hence the name. The marionberry is a cross between the Chehalem and the Olallie blackberry.

Growing season for the marionberry is a short one. When it arrives, I create all things marionberry, such as these sweet and tender Marionberry Streusel Muffins. If you can't find marionberries, blackberries will work just as well.

For the Streusel

⅓ cup all-purpose flour

⅓ cup dark brown sugar

1 teaspoon cinnamon

½ teaspoon ginger

3 tablespoons cold unsalted butter, diced

For the Muffins

1½ cups all-purpose flour

1½ teaspoons baking powder

½ teaspoon baking soda

½ teaspoon salt

1 teaspoon ground nutmeg

8 tablespoons (1 stick) unsalted butter, room temperature

¾ cup granulated sugar

1 egg, room temperature

½ cup buttermilk

2 teaspoons vanilla extract

1 cup (8 ounces) fresh marionberries (or blackberries), tossed with 1 tablespoon flour

1. Preheat the oven to 400°F.

2. To make the streusel, add the flour, brown sugar, cinnamon, and ginger to a small bowl. Cut in the butter until the mixture feels like dry crumbles.

3. To make the muffins, mix together the flour, baking powder, baking soda, salt, and nutmeg.

4. In an electric mixer or by hand, mix together the butter and sugar until nice and creamy, about 5 minutes.

5. Whisk the egg into the creamed mixture. Once the egg is nicely incorporated, slowly add the buttermilk and vanilla extract.

6. Gently fold the dry ingredients into the wet ingredients until combined. Be careful not to overmix or you'll have tough muffins.

7. Fold in the flour-coated fresh marionberries or blackberries if you can't find marionberries. (This recipe also works well with raspberries.)

8. Line a 12-cup muffin tin with muffin cups, and then divide the batter between the 12 muffin wells, filling the muffin cups about ⅔ full. Place a teaspoon or two of streusel on top of the muffin batter.

9. Bake in the oven for 25 to 30 minutes or until the muffins are golden on top.

10. Remove the muffins from the oven and let them cool for 10 to 15 minutes before serving.

Rose Petal Jelly

MAKES TWO 8-OUNCE JARS

Rose Petal Jelly tastes as enchanting as it smells. It's fragrant, slightly sweet, and the prettiest shade of pinkish red. I adore this jelly with Lavender Cream Biscuits (page 15), my morning toast, freshly baked scones, pancakes, waffles, and French toast.

Although you can purchase dried rose petals online, I love to source them locally from farms such as Witte Flower Farm.

I use Pomona's Universal Pectin in this recipe. After testing the recipe three times, Pomona's allowed the jelly to set more firmly than regular powdered pectin, without added sugar. Citrus pectin also allows me to adjust the firmness of the jelly by adding more or less of the pectin. Pomona's Universal Pectin can be found at most local markets; however, it can also be purchased online.

2 cups organic, culinary dried rose petals

3 cups filtered water

1 teaspoon calcium water (from calcium powder included in Pomona's Pectin box)

1 tablespoon rose water

1 tablespoon lemon juice

2 cups granulated sugar

2 teaspoons Pomona's Universal Pectin

Before beginning, sterilize jars and lids according to canning directions.

1. Place the rose petals in a pot, add water, and give it a stir. Bring water to a boil and then turn the heat down to a simmer and cover. Simmer covered on low for 30 minutes.

2. Strain the rose petals and reserve the liquid. I usually end up with about 1½ cups liquid. Prepare the calcium water by combining ½ teaspoon calcium powder (included in pectin box) and ½ cup water in a lidded jar. Shake well.

3. Transfer the rose liquid back to the pot over medium heat and stir in 1 teaspoon of calcium water (reserve the rest for another batch of jelly), rose water, and lemon juice. Combine the sugar with the 2 teaspoons pectin.

4. Bring the liquid to a boil and whisk in the sugar and pectin, continuing to whisk until the liquid comes back to a full boil and the pectin has dissolved.

5. Take the pot off the heat and ladle the jelly into sterilized jelly jars, about three-quarters full. Wipe the rims clean and screw on the lids. Place them in the refrigerator. The jelly will last about 7 days.

Note: If I'm giving the jelly as gifts, I place the filled jars in boiling water that covers the jars, and boil for about 10 minutes. Remove from water and let the jars cool. Check the seals—the lids should have been sucked down.

WITTE FLOWER FARM

KRISTIN LAMONT AND MIKE WITTE / SALEM, OREGON

Located on a tranquil hillside just outside of Salem, Oregon, Witte Flower Farm is a vision of color and beauty with an ever-changing floral landscape during flower season. This enchanting flower farm sits on a hillside with stunning views of Mount Jefferson to the east and the lush green mid-Willamette Valley below.

Witte Flower Farm is the result of creative flower farmer and floral designer Kristin LaMont's hard work. When Kristin and her husband Mike began the farm, they wanted to grow beautiful and fragrant flowers with the best soil possible. The farm is teeming with life and fed with cover crops and compost. They practice a no-till method to protect the complex ecosystem just below the soil's surface. Above the ground, they work to create the healthiest habitat for beneficial insects, pollinators, and the abundance of bird species found in this area.

Kristin grows some of the most beautiful flower varietals, from hard-to-find seed sources around the world. She harvests the flowers during the early-morning light and then bundles the beautiful blooms for sale to florists, wedding designers, Portland Flower Market, and direct online sales with limited shipping.

Throughout flower season, Kristin also hosts floral design workshops, farm visits, and farm-to-table dinners that are prepared by local chefs, farmers, and food artisans. These are truly special events that Kristin enjoys. She cherishes the beauty cultivated on her flower farm and loves to share it with her community. Kristin says, "Come to the farm. A place to be wild. A place to be quiet. A place to belong." After walking the Witte Flower Farm one spring morning, I couldn't agree more. Tranquility abounds, as does Kristin's passion for and commitment to the most beautiful and fragrant flowers.

Apple Butter Baked French Toast

SERVES 6 TO 8

There is no doubt that baked French toast makes a delightful weekend breakfast or brunch. In this recipe, I use cinnamon raisin bread layered with apple butter. It's baked in a creamy custard and served with sweet, sautéed Oregon apples and a pumpkin-pie–spiced whipped cream.

If you don't want to serve it with the apples and whipped cream, a side of maple syrup will be just as delicious.

For the French Toast

2 tablespoons unsalted butter

1 cup apple butter

12 slices cinnamon raisin bread (stale or dry is best)

6 eggs

1½ cups heavy cream

½ cup whole milk

2 teaspoons pumpkin pie spice

Pinch of salt

½ cup maple syrup

For the Brown Sugar Apples

2 apples, sliced

1 tablespoon unsalted butter

¼ cup brown sugar

For the Spiced Whipped Cream

1 pint heavy cream

¼ cup powdered sugar, plus more for garnish

1 teaspoon pumpkin pie spice

1. Use the butter to grease an 8-by-8-by-2-inch baking dish. You can also make this in a larger baking dish using only two layers (as opposed to the three layers you'd make in the 8-inch square baking dish).

2. Spread apple butter onto 4 slices of cinnamon raisin bread., using about 1 tablespoon of apple butter per slice. Place apple-buttered bread side by side on the bottom of the baking dish. Top each slice of apple-buttered bread with one more slice of cinnamon raisin bread.

3. Spread those slices of bread with the remaining apple butter and then top with the remaining four bread slices.

4. Whisk together eggs, heavy cream, whole milk, pumpkin pie spice, salt, and maple syrup. Pour this mixture carefully over the bread in the baking dish, pressing down on the bread a bit to help it absorb the liquid. Cover the baking dish with aluminum foil and place it in the refrigerator overnight or for at least 6 to 8 hours.

5. To bake the French toast, remove it from the refrigerator at least 30 minutes prior to baking.

6. Preheat the oven to 350°F. Place the foil-covered baking dish into the oven and bake for about 1 hour. Take the foil off the baked French toast and let it bake for another 15 minutes uncovered.

7. Remove the dish from the oven and let it sit for about 15 minutes.

8. While the French toast is baking, prepare the brown sugar apples. Add apples, butter, and brown sugar to a saucepan and heat over medium-low heat. Stir the apples and brown sugar until they're nicely combined and the apples are wilting, about 5 minutes. Turn the heat to low and continue to cook and stir often until the apples are soft and glazed with the brown sugar. Remove them from the heat and set aside.

9. Make the spiced whipped cream. In an electric mixer, add the heavy cream, powdered sugar, and pumpkin pie spice. Whisk until fluffy and soft peaks form in the whipped cream. Chill until needed.

10. When ready to serve, dust the Apple Butter Baked French Toast with powdered sugar and serve with the brown sugar apples and spiced whipped cream.

Pear and Cardamom Cobbler

SERVES 6 TO 8

In addition to being Oregon's state fruit, pears are also one of Oregon's top-producing tree fruits. While most of the state's pears are grown in the Hood River region or southern Oregon in Rogue Valley, they can also be found growing on small family farms throughout the Willamette Valley.

Pears are excellent for both sweet and savory recipes, but I especially adore pears when combined with fragrant cardamom. This Pear and Cardamom Cobbler is prepared a little differently than traditional cobblers. The biscuit dough is placed on the bottom of the baking dish and the pears are layered on top. It's a simple recipe that is both flavorful and fragrant.

For the Biscuit Dough

1½ cups all-purpose flour

½ cup coconut sugar (or granulated)

2 teaspoons baking powder

½ teaspoon salt

1 teaspoon ground cardamom

8 tablespoons (1 stick) cold unsalted butter, diced

1 egg, cold

¾ to 1 cup heavy cream, cold

For the Cobbler

¼ cup brown sugar

2 teaspoons ground cardamom

2 to 3 ripe pears, cored and sliced

1 tablespoon cold unsalted butter, diced

Powdered sugar, for garnish, or serve with
    vanilla bean ice cream

1. Preheat the oven to 350°F.

2. To prepare the dough, whisk together the flour, sugar, baking powder, salt, and cardamom in a large bowl. Cut in the diced butter with a pastry cutter or fork or even your fingers until the flour mixture is crumbly. Once the butter is cut into the flour mixture, stir in the egg and ¾ cup heavy cream, just until nicely blended. Add the additional ¼ cup cream if your mixture hasn't reached dough consistency.

3. Press the dough into the bottom of a greased 9-by-13-inch baking dish or a 9-inch round cake pan.

4. To prepare the cobbler, mix together the brown sugar and cardamom in a small bowl. Place the pear slices over the dough in the baking dish or cake pan and sprinkle the brown sugar and cardamom evenly over the top. Place the butter over the pears.

5. Bake for 25 to 30 minutes, or until the cobbler is golden brown. Remove it from the oven and let it cool slightly before serving.

6. Garnish with powdered sugar or serve with vanilla bean ice cream.

Note: I used Bosc pears for my cobbler, but you can use any type of pear you've got on hand or find at your farmers' market. Cardamom is most fragrant and flavorful when it's fresh. If your cardamom has been in your pantry longer than 6 months, you may want to use a teaspoon more in the cobbler or purchase a fresh bottle of cardamom. There is nothing like fresh cardamom in a baked recipe!

Chai-Spiced Pumpkin Coffee Cake

SERVES 8

Because I adore nothing more than a creamy Chai latte on a cool Oregon fall morning, I wanted to create a coffee cake that includes these festive flavors. Not only is the coffee cake infused with the taste of chai spices and Oregon pumpkin, but I've added them to the streusel as well. This is truly a delicious and fragrant coffee cake that will delight the senses and satiate the palate.

This cake would never have had the luxurious crumb without the assistance of my friend Chef Laurie Pfalzer, author of the book *Simple Fruit*. Chef Laurie is a baking and pastry instructor in Seattle and the resource for all my perplexing baking questions.

1 tablespoon butter, for greasing

For the Coffee Cake Topping

⅓ cup all-purpose flour

⅓ cup brown sugar

¼ teaspoon ground ginger

½ teaspoon ground cinnamon

½ teaspoon ground cardamom

5 tablespoons cold unsalted butter, diced

For the Coffee Cake

1½ cups self-rising flour

1 teaspoon cinnamon

1 teaspoon cardamom

½ teaspoon ground ginger

½ teaspoon allspice

4 tablespoons unsalted butter, melted

¾ cup granulated sugar

1 egg

1 cup pumpkin puree

¼ cup buttermilk

1. Preheat the oven to 350°F. Butter an 8-by-8-by-2-inch baking dish.

2. To make the coffee cake topping, mix together the all-purpose flour, brown sugar, ginger, cinnamon, and cardamom in a small bowl. Cut in butter using a fork, pastry cutter, or your hands.

3. To make the coffee cake, mix together flour, cinnamon, cardamom, ginger, and allspice in a medium bowl.

4. In an electric mixer, add the melted butter and sugar and mix to combine. Add the egg, pumpkin puree, and buttermilk and mix thoroughly.

5. Gently mix in the flour and spices just until nicely combined. Pour batter into greased baking dish and sprinkle the topping over the batter.

6. Place the baking dish in the oven and bake for 35 to 45 minutes, until the center is firm to the touch. Once the cake is done, remove it from the oven and let it cool. Serve slightly warm.

FIDDLEHEAD FARM

KATIE COPPOLETTA AND TAYNE REEVE / CORBETT, OREGON

Katie Coppoletta and Tayne Reeve are first-generation farmers and the women behind Fiddlehead Farm in Corbett, Oregon. They didn't grow up farming, and came into agriculture separately during their early twenties. Katie says, "We were both drawn to the physical and rewarding work of farming."

Fiddlehead Farm was started in 2009 with only a few crops and a small plot of land. Over time, Katie and Tayne have worked purposefully to grow the farm not only in acreage but in crop diversity as well. Fiddlehead Farm is certified organic by Oregon Tilth and has expanded to include growing more than 200 varieties of mixed vegetables on five acres of land, with a small orchard to boot.

Katie and Tayne both appreciate how important it is to take care of the earth. They are dedicated to resource conservation; as farmers, they strive to make this a focus in the way they develop the land and their business.

They've installed hedgerows for native pollinators and wildlife, use cover cropping and mulches to protect the soil, and reduce their water usage with drip irrigations. In the future, they hope to install solar panels and rainwater catchment systems.

They also participate in the Rogue Farm Corps, which is a program dedicated to training the next generation of farmers. Katie says, "As mentors in this program, we teach our interns the skills needed to start their own farming operations and strive to show them the value of working with the land and the seasons."

Katie and Tayne believe their success has been due to their fervent love for the work they do and the determination to feed their community high-quality, flavorful food from the earth.

Broccoli and Cheese Pie

SERVES 6

I feel fortunate that my daughters have always liked most vegetables. But their favorite is broccoli. I cannot count the times broccoli with Cheddar sauce was the side dish of choice for our weeknight meals, which is why I created this Broccoli and Cheese Pie. Broccoli is also one of the many fresh and seasonal produce items you'll find at the beautiful Fiddlehead Farm in Corbett, Oregon.

This is actually a crustless quiche, but I knew my kids would eat it if I called it Broccoli and Cheese Pie. It has all the lovely flavors of broccoli and cheese, but it's combined with the lush texture of a savory, quiche-like custard. Cheesy and filled with broccoli, this has become my go-to lunch or brunch recipe. And on occasion, a last-minute dinner recipe.

1 tablespoon unsalted butter

1 tablespoon extra virgin olive oil

1 medium shallot or ½ medium yellow onion, diced

1 clove garlic, minced

½ teaspoon dried thyme (crush it a bit between your fingers)

½ teaspoon dried oregano

1 tablespoon finely chopped fresh parsley

2 cups steamed chopped broccoli

2 cups shredded Swiss cheese

4 eggs

1¾ cups heavy cream

1 teaspoon salt

½ teaspoon black pepper

1. Preheat the oven to 350°F.

2. Butter a 9-inch square deep-dish pie plate and place the pie plate on a baking sheet. This will help prevent any liquid spilling onto the oven floor.

3. In a sauté pan over medium heat, add the olive oil. When the oil is hot, add the shallot or onion and cook for 2 to 3 minutes, or until it's soft and translucent. Stir in the garlic, dried thyme, dried oregano, and fresh parsley. Cook for 1 minute.

4. Take the sauté pan off the heat and toss the onion and herb mixture with the steamed broccoli. Add the broccoli to the bottom of the buttered pie plate.

5. Top the broccoli with the shredded cheese.

6. Whisk together the eggs, heavy cream, salt, and pepper and pour it over the cheese and broccoli.

7. Place the baking sheet with the pie plate into the center of the preheated oven. Bake for 45 to 60 minutes. The pie will be done when the center is springy to the touch.

8. Remove the Broccoli and Cheese Pie from the oven and let it cool for about 15 minutes. Serve this delicious pie with a side of fresh seasonal fruit and mimosas.

Apricot Jam and Goat Cheese Tarts

MAKES 8 TARTS

Summer in Oregon is stone fruit season, and it's the season when I end up with flats of fresh fruit all over my kitchen table. What we don't eat right out of the flat or kitchen fruit bowl usually goes into various breakfast and dessert recipes or sometimes a dinner recipe, and the rest is used for jam.

Apricot jam and goat cheese make a delicious pairing in this crisp and buttery tart. The apricot jam is easily swapped with your favorite fruit jam. That said, I have an affinity for apricot jam served with goat cheese.

2 sheets puff pastry, thawed

1 egg, whisked with 1 teaspoon water

8 ounces apricot jam

4 ounces goat cheese

1. Preheat the oven to 425°F.

2. Cut each pastry sheet into 4 squares and place them on a parchment paper–lined baking sheet. You will have 8 squares total.

3. With a small knife, 1 inch from the edge, score the inside of each square three-quarters of the way through. Do not cut all the way through the puff pastry. Brush the edges of the pastry squares with the egg wash and then place the baking sheet into the oven and bake for about 15 minutes.

4. Remove the pastry sheets from the oven and press down on the inner square to create a well. Add a tablespoon or two of jam into the center of each square and top with goat cheese. Place the baking sheet back into the oven and bake the pastry for another 5 to 10 minutes or until the pastry edges are golden and the cheese has melted.

5. Remove the baking sheet from the oven and let the pastry cool for 5 to 10 minutes. Serve slightly warm.

Savory Beer Bread with Garlic, Cheddar, and Fresh Herbs

MAKES 1 LOAF

Craft beer is a notable part of the Oregon food and beverage culture. Bend, Oregon, leads the way among U.S. cities for the most microbreweries and Oregon ranks fourth in the United States for the most craft breweries per capita. I think it's clear that we love our craft beer here.

Like many, I enjoy sipping a pint of craft beer, especially if it's laced with citrus or fresh herbs. I also love making this savory beer bread recipe. This is the bread I serve with a weekend breakfast instead of biscuits, or I use it as an edible base for fried or poached eggs.

Butter, for greasing

3 cups self-rising flour, using the spoon-and-level method

1 tablespoon granulated sugar

1 large clove garlic, minced

⅔ cup grated Cheddar

1 tablespoon chopped fresh herbs, such as chives, rosemary, and parsley

12 ounces beer (a lager is best in this recipe)

8 tablespoons (1 stick) unsalted butter, melted

1. Preheat the oven to 350°F. Lightly butter a 9-by-5-by-2½-inch loaf pan (this is the standard size).

2. For the self-rising flour, be sure to spoon it gently into the measuring cup. Otherwise, you'll end up with a very dense, tough, biscuit-like bread. Don't dip the measuring cup into the bag of flour.

3. In a large bowl, whisk together flour, sugar, garlic, Cheddar, and fresh herbs. Gently mix together dry ingredients and the beer until combined. Don't overwork the batter.

4. Pour the batter into a greased loaf pan and then pour the melted butter over the top of the batter.

5. Bake for 50 to 60 minutes, until the top is slightly golden brown. Remove the baking pan from the oven and let the bread cool for about 10 minutes before slicing.

Spinach, Pesto, and Ricotta Frittata

SERVES 6 TO 8

A frittata is a delicious way to highlight most seasonal vegetables, which is exactly what I did with the two bags of lovely produce generously given to me by Carri and Jeff of Pitchfork and Crow Farm.

I love to make frittatas year-round and I typically use whatever I have on hand or what I've gotten from my local farmers. Although I use spinach in this recipe, I often substitute with other local and seasonal greens. Oregon has a perfect climate for growing leafy greens, so a large portion of my vegetable purchases at farm stores and farmers' markets are various types of kale, Swiss chard, collards, chicory, and dandelion.

The ricotta gives this recipe a lovely creaminess without being too heavy, and the basil pesto nicely enhances the overall flavor.

8 large eggs

1 cup whole-milk ricotta

½ cup grated Swiss cheese

½ teaspoon salt

½ teaspoon black pepper

2 tablespoons basil pesto

1 tablespoon extra virgin olive oil

1 small yellow onion, diced

6 ounces chopped fresh spinach or baby spinach

6 to 8 fresh basil leaves, torn

Homemade tomato sauce or fresh-sliced tomatoes, for garnish

1. Preheat the oven to 350°F.

2. Whisk together the eggs, ricotta, Swiss cheese, salt, pepper, and basil pesto.

3. In an ovenproof 10- to 12-inch skillet, add olive oil over medium heat. Add the onion and cook until the onion is translucent. Stir in the spinach (in batches if you need to) and cook just until wilted.

4. Pour the egg and ricotta mixture over the spinach and onions and let the frittata set over the heat, 2 to 3 minutes.

5. Place the skillet in the oven and bake for 10 to 15 minutes, or until the center is firm. Remove the skillet from the oven and sprinkle with the basil.

6. Serve warm with a side of homemade tomato sauce or fresh-sliced tomatoes.

PITCHFORK AND CROW FARM

CARRI HEISLER AND JEFF BRAMLETT / LEBANON, OREGON

"Life, liberty, and the pursuit of vegetables!" is the slogan you'll read when you first arrive at the Pitchfork and Crow website. The catchphrase caught my eye and made me smile.

As I wandered this small and charming organic farm located in Lebanon, Oregon, I couldn't help but feel the love and care that goes into growing all the beautiful food. The farm is a picture of lush greens and brightly colored vegetables that dot the rolling landscape. At the center, farmer Carri has planted a row of flowers for something pretty to look at. And a giant old oak tree is poised majestically at the edge of the property.

Pitchfork and Crow is the result of many years of hard work by a husband-and-wife team Jeff and Carri. Although they don't see themselves as agricultural experts, they are both passionate about growing clean, sustainable food while keeping the land rich with vital nutrients.

Carri and Jeff didn't begin as farmers, but after careers in geographic data management and special education, they found themselves immersed in farm life.

As of 2020, Pitchfork and Crow is now in its 12th year and is an Oregon Tilth–certified 15-acre farm. Carri and Jeff practice sustainable and organic farming by rotating vegetable families throughout the fields and focusing on heirloom and open-pollinated varieties and local seed sources. They also manage roughly an acre of established fruit trees on the farm, including many varieties of apples, pears, and plums.

The farm grows produce for their CSA (community supported agriculture) members with pick-up locations in Salem and Lebanon.

According to Carri and Jeff, "Our goal is to provide fresh, organic vegetables while cultivating a lifestyle in harmony with nature and our values of respect for labor, craftsmanship, and community."

Apple, Bacon, and Cheddar Bread Pudding

SERVES 6 TO 8

Apples, bacon, and Cheddar are a mouthwatering combination of sweet and savory flavors, which is why I've paired them in this bread pudding. It's a festive and flavorful dish that is perfect for mornings with family and friends.

I've listed 2 teaspoons salt; however, the local bacon I purchase is uncured with no nitrates, so it's not very salty. If your bacon is salty, I suggest using 1 teaspoon salt instead.

1 tablespoon unsalted butter

12 ounces bacon, cooked and coarsely chopped (reserve 2 tablespoons bacon drippings)

1 small or medium sweet onion, diced

1 teaspoon chopped fresh thyme

1 tablespoon chopped fresh chives

2 cloves garlic, minced

1 medium apple, peeled and diced (about 1½ cups)

2 tablespoons brown sugar

4 cups (packed) stale country white or buttermilk bread, cubed or hand torn (the drier the better)

2½ cups shredded Cheddar, plus ½ cup for the top of the pudding

6 eggs

2 cups half-and-half

2 teaspoons salt

½ teaspoon black pepper

½ teaspoon cinnamon

½ teaspoon ground nutmeg

Serve with real maple syrup, if desired

1. Butter an 8-by-8-by-2-inch baking dish.

2. Add the bacon drippings to a skillet and heat over medium heat. Sauté diced onions until soft and golden. Stir in the fresh thyme, chives, garlic, apple, and brown sugar and cook 1 to 2 minutes longer.

3. Place half the bread (2 cups packed) into the bottom of the baking dish.

4. Sprinkle half the bacon, half the onion-apple mixture, and 1¼ cups shredded cheese over the bread. Place the remaining bread on top of the ingredients in the baking dish and repeat with the remaining bacon, onion-apple mixture, and 1¼ cups shredded cheese. Press down to keep all ingredients in the baking dish.

5. Whisk together eggs, half-and-half, salt, black pepper, cinnamon, and nutmeg. Slowly pour the mixture over the top of the ingredients and press down a bit to be sure the liquid is evenly distributed. Top the bread pudding with the remaining ½ cup shredded Cheddar.

6. Cover the baking dish with foil and place it in the refrigerator overnight.

7. When ready to bake, remove the bread pudding from the refrigerator at least 30 to 45 minutes prior to baking. Bringing the pudding to room temperature before baking will ensure that it bakes evenly.

8. To bake, preheat the oven to 350°F. I place my foil-covered baking dish on a baking sheet just in case any liquid escapes. It'll catch on the baking sheet and not the bottom of my oven.

9. Place the foil-covered baking dish in the oven and bake for about 1 hour. Remove the foil from the baking dish and allow it to bake for another 10 to 15 minutes or until the center of the bread pudding is springy to the touch and the top is golden.

10. When the pudding is done, remove it from the oven and let it rest for about 15 minutes. Serve with a side of maple syrup if desired.

BERMUDEZ FAMILY FARM

DALLAS, OREGON

Growing food and flowers has always been a part of Malinda Bermudez's life. After joining the horticulture club and FFA in high school, Malinda decided to make a career out of her love of growing and earned her degree in horticulture from OSU in Corvallis, Oregon.

Luckily, Malinda married into a family that shares her passion for farming and, in 1997, the Bermudez Family Farm began. They started with just 10 acres south of Independence, Oregon, growing produce for the local community. In 2012, they expanded the farm with another 26 acres between Monmouth and Dallas, Oregon.

Today, this family farm is devoted to growing high-quality local plants, produce, poultry, and flowers for sale at local farmers' markets, a buyer's club, and as part of a CSA (community supported agriculture) membership.

After visiting Malinda and the Bermudez Family Farm, it's evident that they are committed to providing the highest quality of pesticide-free produce, meat, and poultry in a way that is sustainable and earth friendly. And although Malinda has seen the small family farm business change over the years, she is fervently committed to adapting their farm to the changing times.

"We've seen a decline in farmers' market sales over the last five years, which meant we had to adjust and rethink how we sell our goods to the public, and we listen closely to what it is that they want. We're here to make a living at what we love, but also to provide our community with the freshest, healthiest food possible."

It's with love and the promise of a healthy, happy future that the Bermudez Family Farm continues to grow beautiful food and flowers for their community. You can find them at the Saturday Market in Independence, Oregon, and on their website and Facebook page.

Jammy Eggs on Toast Muffins

MAKES 4

There is something about stopping at the farmers' market for eggs that completely delights my farm-loving heart. Eggs that are produced by healthy, happy chickens on farms (such as our local Bermudez Family Farm) have the most gorgeous bright orange yolks and make the most delicious recipes.

For me, a jammy egg is somewhere between a runny yolk and hard-boiled. It spreads easily like jam and makes my toast a delicious morning treat.

Because my family shares my affinity for eggs that are jammy in texture, I created this more travel-friendly recipe, which bakes up much like a muffin. It's a recipe that can be adapted using different kinds of cheese, fresh herbs, and even the addition of ham or bacon.

4 slices of bread, crusts removed (white bread or sourdough works best here)

1 tablespoon unsalted butter, olive oil, or avocado oil, for greasing

4 eggs

Salt and pepper

½ cup shredded cheese (I use Cheddar or Swiss)

¼ cup sliced green onions

Avocado slices, fresh sprouts, and sour cream or salsa

1. Preheat the oven to 375°F.

2. With a rolling pin, roll over each slice of bread to flatten it out and make it pliable. Brush or spray each muffin tin with butter or oil.

3. Gently place and press a slice of flattened bread into each muffin bin. Crack an egg into each crust, sprinkle with some salt and pepper, and top with shredded cheese and sliced green onions.

4. Place the muffin tin in the oven and bake for 12 to 15 minutes or until the eggs are done to your preference. Cooking longer will produce more of a hard-boiled egg texture.

5. Remove the muffin tin from the oven and let the muffins cool for a few minutes. Serve with avocado slices, fresh sprouts, and dollops of sour cream or salsa.

Apple Gingerbread Baked Oatmeal

SERVES 6 TO 8

When my oldest daughter was little, we made several trips every fall to our local U-pick apple farm. She delighted in getting all bundled up in layers of sweaters, her fuchsia winter coat, and matching wellies. I still have vivid memories of her little blonde head swinging back and forth as she sang and danced her way through the apple orchards. I adore any opportunity to be outside walking a farm and collecting fresh produce, but I must admit that seeing the pure joy on my daughter's face was what I loved most.

We always came home with bushels of apples. We ate them fresh, we baked them with cinnamon and sugar, we made apple pie, and we always whipped up some apple pie baked oatmeal. As my family got older, I changed my apple pie baked oatmeal to include my love of all things gingerbread. This recipe is fragrant, slightly sweet, slightly spiced, creamy, and filled with farm-fresh apples. The perfect beginning to any day.

1 tablespoon unsalted butter

2 cups rolled oats

1 teaspoon baking powder

1 teaspoon ground cinnamon

1 teaspoon ground ginger

½ teaspoon ground nutmeg

½ teaspoon salt

¼ teaspoon cloves

⅓ cup brown sugar

2 eggs

3 cups whole milk or alternative milk

2 tablespoons molasses

4 tablespoons butter, melted, or ¼ cup melted coconut oil

2 cups diced fresh apples (no need to peel the apples)

Serve with maple syrup or whipped cream

1. Preheat the oven 350°F. Grease an 8-by-11-inch or 9-inch square baking dish with the butter.

2. In a large bowl, mix together the oats, baking powder, cinnamon, ginger, nutmeg, salt, cloves, and brown sugar.

3. In another large bowl, whisk together the eggs, milk, molasses, and melted butter. Add the oats to the milk and then fold in the apples.

4. Pour the mixture into the baking dish, place the baking dish in the oven, and bake for 45 to 50 minutes, or until the baked oatmeal is firm. Remove the baking dish from the oven and let it cool for about 10 minutes.

5. Serve warm with maple syrup or whipped cream.

Smoked Salmon Hash with Fried Eggs

SERVES 4 TO 6

Chinook Salmon, also known as King Salmon, is the official state fish of Oregon. So naturally, salmon makes it into almost every meal of the day, including breakfast.

In this recipe, smoked salmon is subtly folded into this flavorful hash and then topped with a fried egg. This is a crowd-pleasing, hearty, and satisfying recipe that makes breakfast or brunch the best part of the day.

4 tablespoons ghee or high-heat oil

1 yellow onion, diced

1 red or green pepper, diced

1 to 2 jalapeños, seeded and minced

1 pound potatoes, cubed

Salt and pepper, to taste

6 to 8 ounces smoked salmon, chopped

¼ cup sliced green onions

½ cup shredded Cheddar (optional)

4 eggs, fried

Serve with lemon wedges, crème fraîche, and sliced avocados

1. In a large skillet over medium heat, add 2 tablespoons ghee or oil. Add diced onion, pepper, and jalapeño. Cook until the vegetables are soft and slightly wilted, about 2 minutes.

2. Stir in the cubed potatoes and the additional 2 tablespoons ghee or oil. This additional oil will help crisp up the potatoes. Season with about ½ teaspoon each salt and pepper. Turn the heat to low and cover with a lid. Cook the potatoes for 20 to 30 minutes, or until they're nicely caramelized. Season to taste with salt and pepper.

3. Stir in the smoked salmon and green onions. Take the pan off the heat and top with shredded Cheddar, if using.

4. Serve with fried eggs, lemon wedges, crème fraîche, and sliced avocados.

Note: To fry an egg, add 1 tablespoon butter to a nonstick pan over medium heat. When the butter is melted, crack an egg directly into the pan (or into a small ramekin and then slide the egg from the ramekin into the pan). Allow the egg white to set, about 1 minute. Nudge the edges of the egg to make sure it's not sticking and can easily move around the pan. Tilt the pan slightly away from you and, using a spatula, scoop the egg and flip it. Let the egg cook for 30 seconds to 1 minute longer. Remove the egg from the pan and serve.

Oregon Cherry, Sautéed Onion, and Goat Cheese Flatbread

SERVES 4 TO 6

I make several flatbread recipes every summer season and they all involve fresh Oregon berries. There is something enchanting about berries and cheese combined with aromatics layered on toasty warm bread. Sometimes I use a yeast dough for my flatbread and other times I use this recipe, which is simple and doesn't require yeast or much rise time.

The flatbread is cooked on the stovetop, layered with all the sweet, savory, and tangy ingredients, and toasted in the oven for a few minutes before serving. It's lovely as a starter or as a light lunch or dinner with a lightly dressed salad. I like to serve it with torn basil leaves; dressed arugula, watercress, and pea shoots are delicious with this recipe as well.

For the Flatbread

1¼ cups all-purpose flour, plus more for dusting

½ teaspoon salt

½ teaspoon baking powder

1 teaspoon granulated sugar

3 tablespoons milk

2 tablespoons unsalted butter

1 clove garlic, minced

1 teaspoon dried chives

¼ cup whole-milk Greek yogurt, room temperature

For the Cherry and Onion Topping

3 tablespoons unsalted butter

1 sweet onion, thinly sliced

1 teaspoon granulated sugar

1 cup fresh cherries, pitted and sliced or halved

Salt and pepper, to taste

6 ounces goat cheese

Torn fresh basil leaves, drizzle of olive oil, and sea salt, for garnish

1. To make the flatbread: In a medium bow, mix together the flour, salt, baking powder, and sugar. In a small saucepan, add the milk, butter, garlic, and chives and heat to just warm, 1 to 2 minutes. You don't want hot liquid, just warm enough to melt the butter. In a large bowl, add the warm milk and butter to the yogurt and mix to combine.

2. Slowly, with a spoon, stir the dry ingredients into the wet ingredients and mix to combine. With your hands, knead the dough in the bowl and then transfer to a lightly floured surface. Continue to knead the dough for a few minutes, adding a little more flour as needed.

3. Place the dough in a lightly floured bowl and place plastic wrap or a damp towel over the bowl. Let the dough sit for at least 30 minutes to 1 hour.

4. While the dough is resting, prepare the cherry and onion topping. In a skillet, heat the butter over medium heat and, when it's melted, add the sliced onions and sugar. Let the onions cook down for about 15 minutes. They should be golden brown and slightly caramelized. Then stir in the fresh cherries and let them cook with the onions for about 5 minutes. Take the skillet off the heat, season to taste with salt and pepper, and reserve.

5. Divide the dough into 4 pieces and shape each piece into a ball. On a lightly floured surface, roll out the dough into a disc and continue to roll it into the shape you want—either square, rectangular, or circular and about ¼-inch thick. It doesn't have to be perfect, which is what makes this recipe so pretty. Place the flatbread on a plate or platter.

6. Preheat the oven to 400°F.

7. Heat a dry skillet over medium heat and pat excess flour off the flatbread. When the skillet is hot, add the flatbread and cook until bubbles form and the bottom is slightly golden. Transfer the flatbread to a baking sheet. Continue with the remaining flatbread.

8. When all the flatbread is done, spread or sprinkle goat cheese on the surface of each flatbread and then top with the cherries and onions. Place the baking sheet in the oven and bake for 5 to 10 minutes, until warm and slightly crispy on the edges.

9. Remove the flatbread from the oven and garnish with fresh torn basil and a drizzle of good quality extra virgin olive oil. Sprinkle with a little sea salt and serve immediately.

Note: Although I've given a recipe for homemade flatbread, you can also use a store-bought flatbread for a quick version. Simply prepare the cherry and onion topping as instructed and then skip to step 8 and bake the flatbread until it's golden brown and the goat cheese is soft and melted, 3 to 5 minutes.

BITES RESTAURANT

FON AND THOMAS GILSTRAP / FOREST GROVE, OREGON

Just outside Portland in Forest Grove, Oregon, Bites Restaurant has been on my restaurant radar since the first time I dined there a few years ago. With dishes on the menu such as house-made Crab Cake Balls, Kimchi Fries, Udon Carbonara, and K-Town Tacos with Korean-marinated beef, Bites Restaurant is a glorious collection of Asian fusion dishes that highlight seasonal, farm-fresh ingredients.

The restaurant is the delicious creation of Fon and Thomas Gilstrap. Their mission was simply to bring good food to Forest Grove and the surrounding community, utilizing a diverse assortment of fresh ingredients. The menu is inspired by their Asian ancestry combined with their love of food from other countries. The results are drool-worthy plates of enticing food that is neither too fussy nor boring, but rather inventive and exciting.

Fon and Thomas have endeavored to create a restaurant that is authentically different—and it shows.

Over the last few years Bites Restaurant has received numerous accolades and press, not only from the local community, but from out of state as well.

With all the success, the Gilstraps remain grateful to the community and felt it was important to give something back. In 2017, they started "Dine and Donate." Each month, they partner with a local non-profit and hold a charity dinner where Bites Restaurant donates 100 percent of the proceeds from the dinner. They are proud to say they've raised more than $10,000 for local charities since 2017.

When I asked Thomas what makes him most proud of Bites Restaurant, he replied, "Everything about this restaurant makes us proud. We strive to support our community by sourcing as many locally grown and farm-fresh ingredients possible for the freshest, best-tasting food possible. We simply wanted to eat really good food and share that good food with our community."

Oregon Shrimp Cakes with Apricot Ginger Sauce

MAKES 10 TO 12 3-INCH CAKES

Crab cakes have always been one of my family's favorite meals, especially when we dine out. I especially adore the crab cake balls at Bites Restaurant. But when dining out isn't an option, I make these shrimp cakes at home.

It's not always easy to find fresh crab, so a few years ago, I started using Oregon shrimp. I can usually find small Oregon shrimp year-round (often called bay shrimp), and, because they are slightly sweet like crab, they make an excellent substitute.

In this recipe, I've called for adding the ingredients to a food processor. This helps the shrimp cakes stick together for panfrying. If you don't have a food processor, be sure to finely chop the ingredients for a somewhat smooth shrimp cake dough.

For the Apricot Ginger Sauce

½ cup apricot preserves

1 teaspoon grated fresh ginger

2 tablespoons Thai sweet chili sauce

¼ cup white wine

For the Shrimp Cakes

1 pound small Oregon shrimp, patted dry with a paper towel and coarsely chopped

½ cup finely chopped green onion (about 3 large green onions)

2 cloves garlic, minced

Zest of 1 lemon (about 1 teaspoon)

2 tablespoons chopped cilantro

1 tablespoon Dijon mustard

1 teaspoon smoked paprika

2 teaspoons chili powder

½ teaspoon salt

½ teaspoon black pepper

1 cup panko bread crumbs

½ cup mayonnaise

1 egg, whisked

Dash of hot sauce (optional)

3 to 4 tablespoons ghee or high-heat oil, for panfrying

Thinly sliced green onions, for garnish

1. To make the sauce: In a small saucepan, heat the preserves, grated ginger, chili sauce, and white wine over medium heat. Let it simmer for a few minutes, then take off the heat. When it cools, it will thicken. Reheat the sauce to thin.

2. To make the shrimp cakes: In a food processor, add the chopped shrimp, green onions, garlic, lemon zest, cilantro, Dijon mustard, smoked paprika, chili powder, salt, pepper, ½ cup panko, mayonnaise, and whisked egg. Add a dash of hot sauce, if desired. Pulse a few times to combine the ingredients. You just want them to be cohesive and a bit sticky, so they will stay together while panfrying. Due to variances in the moisture of bay shrimp, adding additional panko or mayonnaise may be needed. Chill in the refrigerator for about 15 minutes.

3. Form 3-inch round patties (making sure they are tightly formed) and place them on a cookie sheet or plate. Place ½ cup panko in a bowl. Heat a large skillet over medium-low heat and add ghee or oil. When the oil is hot, but not smoking, gently dredge shrimp cakes in the panko so they're coated on both sides, and then add them to the skillet. Cook 4 at a time in the skillet. Cook for 2 to 3 minutes on each side, or until both sides are golden brown. Transfer to a paper towel–lined plate or cooling rack.

4. Arrange the shrimp cakes on a platter and garnish with thinly sliced green onion. Serve with the Apricot Ginger Sauce.

Sweet Pea and Feta Fritters with Chive Oil and Sour Cream

MAKES 10 TO 12 3-INCH FRITTERS

Late spring and early summer Oregon boasts a plethora of fresh sweet peas. Peas harvested during this time are sweet and tender and make the most delicious little fritter when combined with feta cheese. To make these fritters even more delicious and fun, I've topped them with a chive oil that adds herby flavors to the fritter and a dollop of sour cream for a cool and creamy finish.

For the Fritters

½ cup self-rising flour

2 eggs

¼ cup whole milk

2 cups peas, cooked (if frozen they need to be thawed)

½ cup thinly sliced green onions

1 medium to large clove garlic, minced

1 tablespoon finely chopped fresh mint

Zest of 1 lemon (about 1 teaspoon)

½ teaspoon salt

½ teaspoon black pepper

½ cup crumbled feta cheese

¼ cup high-heat cooking oil, for frying

Sour cream, to serve

For the Chive Oil

1 bunch chives

½ cup extra virgin olive oil

¼ teaspoon salt

1. For the fritters, whisk together the self-rising flour, eggs, and milk.

2. Place the peas in a bowl, mash them, and stir in the green onions, garlic, chopped mint, lemon zest, salt, pepper, and feta cheese. Then mix the peas into the flour-egg batter.

3. Heat ¼ cup high-heat cooking oil in a skillet over medium-low heat. When the oil is hot, place about one mounded tablespoon per fritter into the pan. If they're thick, pat them down a bit. Don't overcrowd the pan. Cook four to five fritters at a time. Cook them for 3 to 4 minutes on each side or until golden brown. Repeat until all the batter is used.

4. To make the Chive Oil, heat a pot with water and bring it to a boil. While the water comes to a boil, fill a large bowl with ice cubes and cold water (this will be used as an ice bath to cool the blanched chives and keep them a vibrant color). When the water has come to a boil, add the chives and blanch them for about 30 seconds. Transfer the chives to the ice bath. Once the chives have cooled, pat them dry with a paper towel and add them to a blender or food processor with the olive oil and salt. Blend until just pureed. Over-blending can turn the oil brown.

5. Place the fritters on a platter and drizzle with Chive Oil and top with sour cream. Serve immediately.

Ground Lamb Sliders with Cucumbers and Spiced Yogurt

MAKES 8 SLIDERS

Although this recipe began as a grilled, delicious, full-size lamb burger, I think it also makes a fun and enticing slider. I've paired the sliders with a spiced yogurt sauce and fresh cucumbers. It makes the dreamiest dish when served with a Youngberg Hill Pinot Noir. Altogether, this is an excellent starter for any gathering, fun weekend lunch, or dinner.

For the Spiced Yogurt

1 cup whole-milk Greek yogurt

½ teaspoon allspice or ground coriander

2 teaspoons chopped fresh mint

For the Sliders

1 pound ground lamb

4 ounces crumbled feta cheese

½ teaspoon dried oregano

½ teaspoon ground cumin

½ teaspoon ground coriander

1 tablespoon fresh lemon juice

1 to 2 cloves garlic, minced

1 teaspoon salt

½ teaspoon black pepper

¼ cup bread crumbs or panko bread crumbs

1 egg, slightly whisked

8 slider buns

For the Garnish

1 cup hummus (optional)

1 cucumber, thinly sliced

Handful of microgreens or watercress leaves

1. To make the Spiced Yogurt, whisk together the Greek yogurt, allspice, and fresh mint. Set aside.

2. To make the sliders, mix together the ground lamb, feta cheese, dried oregano, ground cumin, ground coriander, fresh lemon juice, minced garlic, salt, pepper, bread crumbs, and whisked egg. Mix lightly or until all the ingredients are evenly incorporated.

3. Divide the ground meat into 8 portions and form small patties. *To grill*, preheat the grill to 375°F. Brush the patties with a little oil and place on the hot grill. Cook for 3 to 4 minutes on each side or until the burgers are cooked through. *To panfry*, heat a large skillet with a tablespoon or two of olive oil over medium heat. When the oil is hot but not smoking, add the burgers and brown on both sides until cooked through. *To bake*, preheat the oven to 375°F. Place the patties on a parchment paper–lined baking sheet and bake in the oven for 8 to 10 minutes, or until they're cooked through.

4. To assemble the burgers, spread a tablespoon of the Spiced Yogurt on one half of a bun and spread the other half with some hummus, if desired. Place the burger on the bottom bun and top with a few thin slices of cucumber, some microgreens or watercress, and then place the top of the bun on the greens. Skewer with a cute party pick to secure. Serve immediately.

Note: If you'd like to prep ahead, prepare the yogurt and burgers the day before and keep in the refrigerator. Just before serving, cook the burgers and assemble. Serve immediately.

Grilled Cheese and Dungeness Crab Salad Sandwiches

MAKES 2 SANDWICHES

I have to admit this is one of my favorite lunch indulgences. It's the lunch I make when I'm hard at work on a project and I simply need something delicious to eat. I decided to add it to the book because honestly, it's just too good not to share. I use fresh Dungeness crab that I get at my local seafood market, but you can use any crab available.

6 to 8 ounces crabmeat, drained and squeezed for excess liquid

2 to 3 tablespoons mayonnaise

4 ounces pimento peppers, drained

1 green onion, minced

1 teaspoon lemon juice

1 teaspoon Dijon or spicy brown mustard

Salt and pepper, to taste

3 tablespoons unsalted butter

4 slices bread

4 slices Cheddar

1. Mix together the crabmeat, mayonnaise, pimento, green onion, lemon juice, and mustard. Season to taste with salt and pepper.

2. Butter one side of each slice of bread. In a skillet over medium-low or low heat, place four slices of bread, buttered side down. Add a slice of cheese to each slice of bread. Then add crab salad to the other two slices of bread and cover with a lid to warm the crab salad and allow the cheese to melt. Adjust the heat as necessary.

3. You want this to be a slow melt so the bread doesn't burn. Once the cheese is soft, flip the two slices of bread without crab salad onto the other two slices of bread with crab salad. Continue to heat slowly until the cheese is melted and the bread is golden brown and toasty. Remove from the skillet and let the sandwiches cool for a few minutes prior to serving.

YOUNGBERG HILL

WAYNE BAILEY / McMINNVILLE, OREGON

The Willamette Valley is home to more than 500 wineries and is known as one of the premier Pinot Noir–producing locations in the world. Among these 500 wineries is a small family estate, grower and producer of Oregon Pinot Noir, Chardonnay, and Pinot Gris: Youngberg Hill.

Youngberg Hill lies in the North Willamette Valley on a serene hillside just outside McMinnville. The views from the tasting room and vineyard are breathtaking and after the first sip of wine, I'd have to agree that the wine is just as impressive.

After a rich and diverse career path, along with many years spent working in the wine industry, Wayne Bailey decided to change careers yet again and become a grape farmer. This led to winemaking, which led to the organic and biodynamic vineyard called Youngberg Hill in 2003. Wayne says he's not just a winemaker but a farmer—a steward of the land and maker of great wine. Wayne Bailey and his family practice holistic farming and natural winemaking to allow their wines to express the natural surroundings and climate where the fruit is grown.

Youngberg Hill is a dry farm, which means no irrigation; instead, the farm is in balance and in sync with nature.

They've also earned third-party sustainable certifications for LIVE and Salmon Safe. In 2010, they were certified "sustainable" by the Oregon Wine Board and in 2018 they were certified organic.

Wayne says, "Our goal is for life on the farm—including the soil, the vines, and all other plant and insect life—to be healthier 50 years from now than today."

Youngberg Hill is a Willamette Valley destination not to be missed. Along with a selection of lush wine, the farm enjoys luxury lodging in the heart of wine country and space for private events and weddings.

Albacore Tuna Ceviche with Chimichurri Sauce

SERVES 4 TO 6

Oregon is fortunate to have fresh seafood year-round, which makes ceviche a regular on our family menu. I love to serve this as a starter when everyone is home for Sunday dinner, or as a light lunch served with warm tortillas.

I was first introduced to chimichurri sauce nearly 18 years ago when my sister-in-law and my brother made it for me while visiting one summer. It was so delicious I could have sipped it! Since that day I have continued to make chimichurri sauce and use it for all sorts of delicious dishes. I think this sauce pairs deliciously with seafood, especially a ceviche. It adds bright flavor and color, giving any meal a festive touch.

For the Ceviche

1 pound fresh, wild albacore tuna, cut into 1-inch cubes or diced

6 to 8 limes (enough lime juice to cover the tuna), divided

1 white onion, diced

1 to 2 jalapeños, seeded and diced

½ cup sweet corn

2 tomatoes, seeded and diced

½ cup chopped cilantro

¼ cup extra virgin olive oil

Salt and pepper, to taste

Chimichurri, fresh avocado slices, and tortilla chips, to serve

For the Chimichurri

3 cloves garlic

½ cup fresh basil leaves

½ cup fresh Italian parsley leaves

1 cup fresh cilantro leaves

3 green onions

Leaves from 2 sprigs fresh oregano

1 teaspoon lemon zest

3 tablespoons fresh lemon juice

1 cup extra virgin olive oil

Salt and pepper, to taste

1. To make the ceviche, add the tuna to a ceramic or glass bowl and cover the tuna with lime juice (keep one lime for use later). Cover the bowl and refrigerate for 8 hours or overnight.

2. To make the chimichurri sauce, add all the ingredients to a blender and puree just until the chimichurri is slightly smooth. It doesn't have to be completely pureed. Season to taste with salt and pepper. Store covered in the refrigerator for up to 3 days.

3. Once the tuna is ready, drain the lime juice. Place the tuna in a ceramic bowl and add the onion, jalapeños, sweet corn, tomatoes, and cilantro. Toss lightly to combine. Then add the juice of one lime and olive oil. Again, toss lightly to combine. Season to taste with salt and pepper.

4. To serve, place a tablespoon or two of chimichurri in small serving bowls, martini glasses, or cocktail glasses and top with ceviche. Drizzle with chimichurri, if desired, or serve it on the side. Serve with avocado slices and tortilla chips.

Summary Melon Salsa

MAKES ABOUT 4 CUPS

We grow quite a variety of melons here in Oregon, and toward the end of the summer, our markets are flooded with a gorgeous array. Some are quite sweet and some are mellow, and there is one heirloom melon that tastes a bit like a banana Laffy Taffy.

Because we have so many varieties of melon, I love to use them in breakfast recipes, for a light snack, as dessert, and in this savory salsa recipe. This recipe is fun to serve as a starter with pita or corn chips, but it also makes the most delicious topping for grilled salmon and white fish, and it pairs well with shrimp or scallops, chicken, and burgers.

3 cups diced assorted melon: cantaloupe, honeydew, watermelon, Crenshaw, Galia, Canary . . .

1 small red onion, diced

2 jalapeños, diced

½ cup chopped cilantro

Squeeze of fresh lime

1 to 2 tablespoons extra virgin olive oil

Pinch of salt

Mix together the melon, red onion, jalapeños, cilantro, lime juice, and olive oil. Season lightly with salt. Serve immediately. Try it with tortilla chips, over grilled fish, or as a salsa for fish tacos.

Note: As the salsa rests, it will weep liquid. Drain excess liquid before serving.

Dressed Chelsea Gem Oysters with Pomegranate, Ginger, and Pickled Serrano

RECIPE FROM CHEF MAYLIN CHAVEZ

MAKES 1⅔ CUPS LIQUID FOR UP TO 4 DOZEN OYSTERS

Chef Maylin Chavez creates the most exquisite oyster recipes at her Oyster Bar pop-ups in Portland, Oregon, and many of her unique recipes are available year-round. She also likes to highlight seasonal recipes that capture the freshest, local ingredients available, like these Chelsea Gem oysters paired with seasonal pomegranates. For a spicy twist, Chef Maylin adds fresh ginger and house-pickled serrano peppers, making this lovely dish a Portland favorite.

Chelsea Gems are the first-tide tumbled oyster and they have a slight minerality and mild brine. This makes the Chelsea Gem a great introductory oyster, which pairs well with the tartness of the pomegranate. This recipe calls for Blood Orange Olive Oil from Temecula Olive Oil Company, which can be ordered from their website. However, feel free to substitute with your favorite olive oil.

continued . . .

For the Pomegranate, Ginger, and Pickled Serrano Dressing

1½ cups **POM or equivalent pomegranate juice**

1 teaspoon **Red Boat or equivalent fish sauce**

Juice of half a lime

1 teaspoon **grated young ginger**

1 teaspoon **grated Olympia Oyster Bar House-Pickled Serrano Peppers (see page 54)**

¼ cup **cooked blended red and white quinoa**

¼ cup **pomegranate seeds (1 seed per oyster)**

½ teaspoon **Temecula Olive Oil Company Blood Orange Oil, or your favorite olive oil**

For the Oysters

2 to 4 dozen **Chelsea Gem oysters from Chelsea Farms, Washington**

Micro basil, 1 leaf per oyster (many farms and markets carry this herb)

2 teaspoons **Temecula Olive Oil Company Blood Orange Oil, or your favorite olive oil, 1 drop per oyster**

1. For the dressing: Combine the pomegranate juice, fish sauce, and lime juice, and set aside.

2. Combine the grated ginger and serrano, and set aside.

3. Heat a skillet to medium heat, add quinoa, and lightly toast until fragrant, about 2 minutes, stirring frequently to prevent it from burning. Set aside.

4. Cut a pomegranate in half and release the seeds, ensuring you do not get any of the pith, as it can be really bitter. Drizzle the ½ teaspoon of blood orange oil over the seeds and toss. Set aside.

5. For the oysters: To shuck your oysters, you will need a towel and an oyster knife.

6. Once you have shucked your oyster and released the oyster from the lower abductor muscle, add 1 teaspoon of the pomegranate mixture and 1 tiny pinch of ginger and serrano at the tip of the oyster. Then sprinkle 3 to 4 quinoa seeds on top and place one leaf of micro basil, and a drop of blood orange oil. Et voilà! You have a fall-inspired dressed oyster on the half shell.

Note: The dressing in this recipe depends on the size of the oysters. Generally speaking, each oyster should get 1 teaspoon of dressing. The recipe should ultimately yield 1⅔ cups of liquid. Feel free to reserve the remaining liquid in the refrigerator for up to 3 days.

CHEF MAYLIN CHAVEZ

PORTLAND, OREGON

Portland boasts a plethora of talented chefs, but there is one chef who has forged a delicious and well-known name in Oregon seafood.

Chef Maylin Chavez, owner of the Olympia Oyster Bar pop-up in Portland, is a native of Tijuana, Baja California Norte. She grew up foraging for clams on the beach, in a family where every kind of local seafood was a staple on the dinner table, and she is always eager to bring her heritage and passion for the sea to each dish she prepares. Her style is very much like the place she grew up—Baja-infused with clean, bright flavors, acidic layers, minimal butter, and no animal fat. Chef Maylin believes her seafood dishes should be complemented by seasonal ingredients rather than hidden by them.

With a diverse culinary career and travels across the globe, Maylin holds impressive street cred. When we met, I thought she might want to talk about her past success, but instead, with a big smile and gracious demeanor, she launched into a warm and inviting conversation about the amazing selection of seafood and oysters here in the Pacific Northwest. I found her to be extremely passionate about her work and her Pacific Northwest community.

Chef Maylin said that her culinary experience and travels have greatly influenced her creativity, but also strengthened her passion for fresh, local seafood. Regarding her cooking style, she says, "My approach to oyster and seafood cookery is to surprise the senses and bring a mélange of globally inspired flavors to each bite you enjoy."

Today, Chef Maylin continues to prepare her creative ocean delicacies at pop-up oyster bars and friendly kitchen takeovers around the greater Portland area. She's also teamed up with Nevør Shellfish Farm and creates her beautiful cuisine at the ultimate oyster pop-up bar on the Oregon coast in Netarts Bay. What truly excites Chef Maylin is creating an inviting space for community to gather and share plates of seasonal seafood that translates into many delicious moments.

Olympia Oyster Bar House-Pickled Serrano Peppers

RECIPE FROM CHEF MAYLIN CHAVEZ

MAKES ABOUT 1 CUP PEPPER RINGS

Chef Maylin Chavez created this lovely recipe to complement many of her seasonal oyster recipes. It's become a staple at her pop-up restaurant, Olympia Oyster Bar. It provides a sweet and spicy finish to the oysters. This recipe calls for pickling spices, but you may also use store-bought pickling spices, if that's more convenient. If using store-bought, add 1 tablespoon for the brine.

These House-Pickled Serrano Peppers are used in Chef Maylin's fall oyster recipe, Dressed Chelsea Gem Oysters with Pomegranate, Ginger, and Pickled Serrano (page 51).

10 serrano peppers

2 cups distilled white vinegar

⅓ cup kosher salt

⅓ cup granulated sugar

1 teaspoon coriander seeds

2 cloves

1 bay leaf

1 teaspoon chili flakes

1 teaspoon black peppercorns

1 teaspoon dried oregano

1. Cut peppers into ¼-inch rings.

2. Bring all remaining ingredients to a boil in a medium saucepan. Reduce the heat to medium and simmer for 5 minutes.

3. Pour hot brine over peppers. Let cool, then refrigerate for 24 hours before using. Store in refrigerator for up to 1 month.

Roasted Apricots with Goat Cheese, Bacon, and Honey

MAKES 16 STUFFED APRICOTS

I used to make this recipe with roasted or grilled Oregon nectarines and peaches. At some point, however, I had a flat of fresh local apricots. Fruit and cheese are always a delicious pairing, especially goat cheese paired with fresh summer apricots. I added bacon to the recipe, which gives it a nice salty and smoky flavor. For a touch of sweetness, I finish this dish with honey. This recipe is perfect for summer entertaining when fresh apricots are at their peak in Oregon.

4 ounces creamy goat cheese

2 tablespoons honey, plus more for garnish

½ teaspoon chopped fresh thyme

8 apricots, halved and pitted

1 tablespoon olive oil

4 ounces bacon, cooked and crumbled

1. Preheat the oven to 350°F.

2. In a small bowl, mix together the goat cheese, honey, and thyme until well combined. Place the goat cheese mixture in a pastry bag with piping tip, or a zip-top bag with one corner cut to pipe out the cheese. Reserve.

3. Place the apricot halves on a baking sheet and brush them with olive oil. Bake the apricots in the oven for 5 to 8 minutes, or until the apricots are slightly soft but not falling apart. Remove the apricots from the oven and set them on a platter.

4. Pipe a teaspoon or two of goat cheese into the center of each apricot. Sprinkle with bacon pieces and then drizzle with additional honey. Serve immediately.

UNGER FARMS

KATHY AND MATT UNGER / CORNELIUS, OREGON

As we drove up the gravel road to Unger Farms in Cornelius, Oregon, on what was my very first visit several summers ago, I was immediately in awe of the beauty surrounding this lovely Oregon farm.

Unger Farms sits on a tranquil hillside that is surrounded by acres of berry plants, a farm store, and a large pond that shimmers in the distance. Kathy and Matt Unger started Unger Farms together in 1984. Matt is a third-generation farmer with a BA in agriculture from Oregon State University (OSU). Unger Farms is a GAP-certified (Good Agricultural Practices) farm and, in 2014, they won the OSU Excellence in Family Business Award.

Along with the help of their four children, the Unger family grows 144 acres of Oregon berries, from blueberries, blackberries, and raspberries to their most popular crop, strawberries. These aren't just any strawberries either. Unger Farms grows some of the sweetest, juiciest strawberries I've ever had the pleasure of tasting. In the spring, strawberries are a U-pick crop, which makes this farm even more fun to visit.

At the center of the farm sits a farm store and cafe. The Berry Café has a list of delicious items on the menu, including berry smoothies, berry-infused desserts, salads, and sandwiches.

The farm store is stocked with a selection of just-picked berries, honey, jams, and local wine. Plus, it includes a charming little gift shop and a deck with outside seating that has the dreamiest view of the landscape.

Kathy says, "It's important to us to grow the freshest, best-tasting produce for our community, as well as provide a place for our visitors to bask in the peace and quiet of the farm."

Roasted Summer Berries on Ricotta Crostini

MAKES 16 TO 20 CROSTINI

Roasting fresh berries intensifies their flavors and makes for a mouthwatering topping over sweet ricotta cheese and crostini. I make this recipe when Oregon berries are sweet and in season or when I've been berry picking or visiting the Berry Café at Unger Farms.

In this recipe, I've added fresh chopped thyme, which creates a hint of herbal, savory flavor and mingles with the sweetness of the berries.

2½ cups grapes and assorted berries (blueberries, sliced strawberries, raspberries, and blackberries)

½ teaspoon chopped fresh thyme

Pinch of salt

¼ cup granulated sugar

1 cup whole-milk ricotta, drained in a mesh strainer for at least 10 minutes

3 tablespoons honey

1 baguette, sliced in ¼- to ½-inch slices

1 tablespoon extra virgin olive oil

Fresh mint, for garnish

1. Preheat the oven to 400°F.

2. In a large bowl, toss the fresh berries with the thyme, salt, and sugar. Transfer the mixture to a baking sheet. Place the baking sheet in the oven and roast for 20 to 25 minutes. Remove the berries from the oven and let them cool.

3. In a medium bowl, mix together the drained ricotta and 2 tablespoons of honey. Reserve.

4. Brush the baguette slices with olive oil and place them in a single layer on a baking sheet. Place them in the preheated oven and toast for about 5 min-utes, just until they are slightly toasted. Remove the baguette slices from the oven and let them cool.

5. Place baguette slices in a single layer on a platter. Top with a dollop of honey-ricotta and a spoonful of roasted berries. Drizzle with the remaining 1 table-spoon of honey. Garnish with fresh mint and serve immediately.

Smokey Blue Cheese Baked Potato Chips

SERVES 4 TO 6

My brother and twin sister are some of the most wonderful humans on this planet. Yes, I adore them. They love food as much as I do and my twin sister is also a chef. This is one of many recipes she has given me over the years. I thought it was a brilliant idea when she first told me about it. Because who wouldn't love pungent and flavorful Rogue Creamery Smokey Blue cheese baked on potato chips? This makes a fun starter for any gathering or a late-night snack with a glass of Oregon Pinot Noir.

6 cups plain, thick-cut potato chips

4 ounces crumbled Rogue Creamery Smokey Blue cheese, or your favorite blue cheese

Thinly sliced green onions, for garnish

1. Heat the oven to 400°F.

2. Place the chips in a single layer on a large parchment paper–lined baking sheet. Sprinkle with the blue cheese. Bake the chips for 8 to 10 minutes or until the blue cheese has melted.

3. Remove them from the oven and let them cool for about 5 minutes before serving. Garnish with thinly sliced green onions.

Rustic Leek Tart with Lemon-Thyme Ricotta

SERVES 6 TO 8 AS AN APPETIZER, OR 4 AS AN ENTRÉE

Leeks are one of Oregon's spring and summer crops, and add a lovely sweet aromatic flavor to recipes. When slowly cooked in butter, leeks become sweet and caramelized and make an enticing addition to a tart. I've added whole-milk ricotta infused with citrus and herbs, which creates a creamy base for the sweet leeks. All of these flavorful ingredients are baked on a buttery and crisp puff pastry.

For the Lemon-Thyme Ricotta

8 ounces whole-milk ricotta, drained in a mesh strainer for 10 minutes

1 teaspoon lemon zest

1 teaspoon coarsely chopped fresh thyme

1 to 2 cloves garlic, minced

¼ cup freshly grated Parmesan

Salt and freshly cracked black pepper, to taste

For the Leek Tart

5 to 6 small to medium leeks

2 tablespoons unsalted butter

1 tablespoon extra virgin olive oil, plus more for brushing

1 sheet puff pastry

1 egg

1 teaspoon cold water

Options for garnish: Handful of pea shoots dressed with lemon juice and olive oil, watercress, arugula, carrot swirls, or edible flowers.

1. Preheat the oven to 425°F.

2. To make the lemon-thyme ricotta: Whisk together the ricotta, lemon zest, fresh thyme leaves, garlic, and grated Parmesan. Season with salt and pepper. Reserve.

3. To make the leek tart: Trim the root ends of the leeks but be sure not to cut the ends completely off, as we want the leeks to stay together during cooking. Then give them a rinse, fanning the layers to remove any trapped dirt. Trim the leeks just at the point where they turn pale green. Slice each leek in half lengthwise.

4. Heat a skillet with the butter and olive oil over medium heat. Just as the butter melts and the butter/oil mixture is hot, add the leeks cut side down. Place a lid over the skillet, turning the heat to medium low if needed, and cook for 2 to 3 minutes. With tongs, gently turn the leeks once and let them cook another 2 to 3 minutes until soft and wilted. You may need a longer cook time for medium or larger leeks.

5. Take the pan off the heat and reserve. Next, line a baking sheet with parchment paper and brush the parchment with a little oil. Unfold the puff pastry and place it on the parchment. Roll it out just a bit, to smooth out the seams, but not too much, as puff pastry needs to be ¼- to ⅓-inch thick to puff. Pierce the puff pastry with a fork several times in all corners and the middle of the pastry.

6. Spread the ricotta mixture evenly over the pastry, leaving a 1-inch border on all sides. Place the butter-braised leeks evenly over the ricotta.

7. Whisk together the egg and cold water to make an egg wash. Brush the edges of the pastry with the egg wash and then place the baking pan in the preheated oven for 20 to 25 minutes, or until the pastry is golden brown.

8. Remove the pastry from the oven and let it cool slightly before slicing.

9. Garnish with a handful of pea shoots dressed with lemon juice and olive oil, watercress, arugula, carrot swirls, or edible flowers. Serve warm.

SOUPS AND STEWS

Creamy Mushroom Soup

SERVES 4

As the end of August approaches, wild mushroom season in Oregon begins. Due to the rainy and cool Pacific Northwest climate and an abundance of forests, wild mushroom season can extend all the way through April. A few varietals such as Black Morels and Spring King Boletes can be found from April through June. If wild mushroom foraging isn't on your list of activities, Oregon has several mushroom farms, such as The Mushroomery, that grow a variety of species of fungi, and they can be found at various farmers' markets throughout the state.

Some of my favorite mushrooms to include in this soup are Pacific Golden Chanterelle, Lobster, Lion's Mane, and Oyster. But if you have limited access to a selection of mushrooms, I'd recommend any brown mushroom or cremini.

I adore this soup à la carte for lunch or dinner, but it also makes a lovely starter to any meal.

2 tablespoons unsalted butter

1 large sweet onion, diced

3 cloves garlic, minced

3 sprigs fresh thyme

1 tablespoon fresh chopped Italian parsley

1 tablespoon fresh chopped dill

1½ pounds fresh mushrooms, sliced or coarsely chopped (assorted mushrooms and cremini)

1 teaspoon paprika

1 cup white wine

2 tablespoons all-purpose flour

3 cups vegetable or chicken broth

½ to 1 cup heavy cream

Salt and pepper, to taste

Chopped fresh parsley, chives, dill, or thyme, for garnish

1. In a soup pot, heat the butter over medium heat and add the onion. Cook until slightly wilted, 2 to 3 minutes. Then stir in the garlic, fresh thyme, parsley, and dill. Cook for 1 minute longer.

2. Add the mushrooms and let them cook for 5 to 8 minutes, or until their liquid has evaporated and the mushrooms become a bit golden or brown in color. Stir in the paprika and white wine and let it simmer for 1 to 2 minutes.

3. Sprinkle the flour over the mushrooms and stir to combine. Let this cook for 1 to 2 minutes and then add the vegetable or chicken broth. Reduce the heat to low and simmer for 12 to 15 minutes, or until the soup has thickened slightly.

4. Stir in ½ cup heavy cream and simmer on low until soup is thickened and is at a desired consistency. Add the additional ½ cup heavy cream if needed. Season to taste with salt and pepper.

5. To serve, ladle soup into bowls and garnish with fresh chopped parsley, chives, dill, or thyme. Serve warm.

Note: For a thicker soup, mix together 1 tablespoon cornstarch and 1 tablespoon cold water. Add this to the simmering soup and let it cook for 1 to 2 minutes until thickened.

THE MUSHROOMERY

JENNIFER MACONE AND DUSTIN OLSEN / LEBANON, OREGON

Have you ever been to a mushroom farm? It's a completely different type of farming, but one that cofounder and owner Jennifer Macone has spent most of her life doing. When Jennifer was 17 years old, she left Miami, Florida, and headed to the West Coast to live closer to nature. She got her wish when, not long after her arrival, she was invited on a wild mushroom hunting trip. That is the moment when she fell in love with mushrooms.

Jennifer's passion for mushrooms led to a degree in mycological studies and then a job working at a local mushroom farm in Washington. There, she learned how to grow and cultivate a variety of mushrooms along with the business of farming. Jennifer continued wild mushroom hunting and foraging, where she met her current business partner, Dustin Olsen.

Dustin and Jennifer started their mushroom farm in Bellingham, Washington, but eventually decided to move to Oregon where the climate is optimal, water is abundant, and they would be surrounded by some of the best wild mushroom hunting grounds in the United States.

Today, The Mushroomery is a family-owned, certified organic farm that grows gourmet and medicinal mushrooms in the foothills of the Cascade Mountains. They create mushroom powders, package wild and cultivated dried mushrooms, prepare medicinal tinctures, and assemble several "grow-your-own" indoor and outdoor mushroom kits.

The Mushroomery uses biodynamic farming practices and they purchase growing mediums from local farmers. Jennifer says, "I am proud that this business was built from scratch by the passion of two people who want to make available organic, healthy, nutritional mushrooms from both farm and forest. The health of people and the earth are our first priority and that is why we started our farm. Also, we love mushrooms!"

Asparagus Leek Soup with Mushroom Gremolata

SERVES 2 TO 3

When we visited Cowhorn Vineyard & Garden in the early summer, they were just finishing up their asparagus harvest. Besides making some of the best wine in Oregon, Cowhorn also grows a bumper crop of asparagus. Inspired by the visit, as soon as we arrived home, I launched myself into making Asparagus Leek Soup.

Spring asparagus and spring leeks are the base for this luscious recipe. It has the prettiest pale green color, and it's slightly creamy with a hint of herbs. It's so delicious I could dive into it face first. Although this soup is just as enjoyable ungarnished, I think it's even better with the mushroom gremolata.

Our wild mushroom season begins just around the time we harvest spring asparagus, making these two Oregon crops a most tasteful pairing.

For the Soup

2 tablespoons unsalted butter

2 medium leeks, white and pale green parts only, halved lengthwise, washed, and chopped

2 cloves garlic, lightly chopped

½ teaspoon dried herbs de Provence, crushed between fingers as you're adding it to the soup

1 teaspoon fresh thyme

2 pounds fresh asparagus, trimmed and chopped into 1-inch pieces

2 cups vegetable broth or as needed for desired consistency

½ to 1 cup heavy cream

Squeeze of lemon

Salt and pepper, to taste

For the Gremolata

1 tablespoon unsalted butter

¼ to ½ cup thin-sliced fresh mushrooms

1 tablespoon chopped fresh Italian parsley

½ teaspoon lemon zest

Salt and pepper, to taste

1. Heat the butter in a medium soup pot over medium heat and add the chopped leeks. Cook the leeks until they are soft and somewhat golden. Stir in the garlic, dried herbs de Provence, and fresh thyme, and cook for 1 minute longer.

2. Stir in the asparagus and 1½ cups broth (add more later if needed) and simmer on low, covered, for 10 to 15 minutes, or until the asparagus is tender.

3. Puree ¾ of the soup with an immersion blender or wait a few minutes for the mixture to cool and then add it to a countertop blender and puree. If using a countertop blender, return the soup to the soup pot over low heat and stir in the heavy cream. While stirring the soup, add the squeeze of lemon juice and season to taste with salt and pepper.

4. Take the soup off the heat and let it sit covered while you prepare the gremolata.

5. In a sauté pan, heat the butter and, when it's hot and frothy, add the mushrooms. Let the mushrooms "toast" in the butter until they are soft and slightly golden. Take the pan off the heat and gently toss the mushrooms with the parsley and lemon zest. Season with salt and pepper to taste.

6. Ladle the soup into bowls and garnish with the mushroom gremolata. Serve immediately.

Note: Judy Niver, one of our talented recipe testers, also recommends serving this soup with homemade croutons. I think this is a delicious idea! See the note on page 86 for instructions to make your own croutons.

Spiced Winter Squash Soup

SERVES 2

My brother lives abroad and, while chatting one day, he mentioned a lovely spiced kabocha squash soup he'd tasted at a dinner party. He described it as silky in texture, slightly sweet in flavor, and simply luscious. At the time, I made a roasted pumpkin soup that sounded similar, but my brother's enthusiastic description inspired me to load up on all types of unique winter squash and test new recipes.

Oregon has a plethora of winter squash available throughout the fall and winter months, so I have tested an endless supply of varieties for this recipe: kabocha, sugar pie pumpkin, butternut, sweet dumpling, buttercup, red kuri, Hubbard, and carnival. They were all delicious, but I definitely lean toward the sweeter squash such as buttercup, butternut, red kuri, and Hubbard.

Winter squash pairs deliciously with spices, so I've added garam masala and cinnamon for a festive and fragrant flavor. This tasty little soup recipe has become a regular on my fall and winter menu, and makes the loveliest lunch soup in the middle of a winter workday.

Although this soup recipe serves two, it's easily doubled and makes a lovely appetizer for dinner guests.

1½ to 2 pounds (or 2 cups cooked and pureed) winter squash: kabocha, pumpkin, acorn, butternut . . .

2 tablespoons coconut oil or butter, plus more for brushing

1 small yellow onion, diced

1 clove garlic, minced

1 teaspoon garam masala

½ teaspoon cinnamon

½ cup chicken or vegetable broth, plus more if needed

½ cup heavy cream

Salt and pepper, to taste

Crème fraîche and a sprinkle of orange zest, for garnish

1. To roast the squash, preheat the oven to 425°F.

2. Slice the squash in half, remove the seeds, brush the flesh (not the skin) with oil, and place the squash flesh side down in a baking dish. Add about 1 inch of water to the bottom of the baking dish. Roast the squash in the oven for 30 to 45 minutes, depending on the thickness of the squash. The squash is done when it's soft.

3. Remove the baking dish from the oven and let the squash cool completely. Remove the skin and add the squash to a blender or food processor. Puree the squash until smooth. Reserve 2 cups of puree for the soup. If you have remaining squash, freeze it for future use.

4. To make the soup, place a soup pot over medium heat and add the coconut oil or butter. Stir in the onions and cook until they are golden, about 5 minutes. Stir in the garlic and let it cook 1 minute longer.

5. Stir in the winter squash puree, garam masala, cinnamon, broth, and heavy cream. Bring to a simmer and turn the heat to low. Simmer for about 5 minutes, adding additional broth or cream as needed for desired consistency. Season to taste with salt and pepper.

6. If you like a smoother soup texture, puree with an immersion blender or add it to a blender and puree until smooth.

7. Garnish with crème fraîche and orange zest. Serve warm.

Slow-Cooked Rosemary and Porcini Beef Stew with Farro

SERVES 4 TO 6

After getting to know the good folks at Nehalem River Ranch, I wanted to create a recipe worthy of their commitment to quality. This recipe highlights the rich taste of grass-fed beef with the fragrant and earthy flavors of rosemary and porcini.

I've paired this beef stew with farro, which is one of our prized Pacific Northwest crops. The nutty taste and slightly chewy texture of farro provides an enticing addition to the medley of ingredients in this stew.

1 ounce dried porcini mushrooms

1 cup boiling water

3 to 4 tablespoons avocado oil, ghee, or another high-heat oil

3 to 3½ pounds beef chuck, cut into bite-size cubes

Salt and pepper, to taste

2 yellow onions, chopped

2 medium carrots, chopped

1 rib celery, diced

6 cloves garlic, diced

1 tablespoon chopped fresh rosemary

1 tablespoon chopped fresh parsley, plus more for garnish

½ teaspoon dried thyme

¼ cup all-purpose flour

1 cup red wine

3 cups beef broth

1 tablespoon tomato paste

2 dried bay leaves

1 to 2 cups water, as needed

1 teaspoon red wine vinegar

1 teaspoon granulated sugar

1 cup farro, cooked according to package directions

1. Preheat the oven to 325°F.

2. Place the dried mushrooms in a heatproof bowl and add the boiling water. Let them steep for about 15 minutes. Once they are soft, strain the mushrooms, reserving at least ½ cup of the mushroom water. Lightly chop the mushrooms into bite-size pieces and reserve.

3. In a Dutch oven or heavy-bottomed ovenproof pot over medium-high heat, add 2 tablespoons of oil. Sprinkle the beef cubes with salt and pepper and, when the oil is hot, add about 1/3 of the beef cubes and brown. Transfer the beef to a platter and repeat with the next two batches of beef, adding additional oil as needed. It's important to add small amounts of beef to the pot at a time so that the beef will brown evenly. If you add too much beef, it will steam instead of brown. It takes a little time, but the browning process translates into a lot of delicious flavor.

4. Once the beef has been browned, turn the heat down to medium and add the onions, carrots, and celery to the pot and cook until softened, 2 to 3 minutes. Add the garlic, rosemary, parsley, and thyme. Cook for 1 minute longer.

5. Stir in the flour and let it cook for 1 minute. Add the beef with any accumulated juices back into the

pot. Stir in the red wine, beef broth, tomato paste, dried bay leaves, porcini mushrooms, and the ½ cup of reserved mushroom liquid. You want to just cover the beef in liquid, so, if needed, add ½ cup of the water at a time. Bring the liquid to a boil. Take the pot off the heat and cover with a tight-fitting lid. Place it in the oven and let it slow cook for about 2 hours. Check the stew after 1 hour and give it a stir.

6. The stew will be done when the meat is fork tender. Remove the pot from the oven and stir in the red wine vinegar and sugar. This will bring all those lovely flavors together. Let the stew cool for at least 10 minutes before serving.

7. Divide the cooked farro among four to six bowls and ladle stew over the farro. Garnish with fresh chopped parsley and serve.

Chorizo and White Bean Stew

SERVES 6

Several farms here in the Willamette Valley make the most delicious Spanish-style chorizo. It's so good, I keep it in my freezer for soups, stews, tacos, and macaroni and cheese. Yes, I put chorizo in my mac and cheese. However, one of my favorite chorizo recipes is this white bean stew. It's a simple stew that comes together quickly, but tastes even better when it's had time to hang out on the stovetop for an hour. For a complete meal, serve with crusty bread to dunk into the stew and a salad of winter greens.

1 to 2 tablespoons extra virgin olive oil or ghee

1 large onion, diced

1 roasted red pepper, diced

2 ribs celery, diced

3 to 4 cloves garlic, minced

1 teaspoon fresh chopped thyme leaves

1 tablespoon fresh chopped parsley

1 tablespoon smoked paprika

4 cups chicken broth, plus more if needed

2 bay leaves

1 pound cooked ground chorizo (fat drained)

Pinch of red pepper flakes (optional, especially if the chorizo is spicy)

Two 15-ounce cans cannellini (white) beans, drained

1 teaspoon white wine vinegar

Salt and pepper, to taste

1. Place a large soup pot over medium heat and add the oil or ghee. When the oil or ghee is hot, add the onion, red pepper, and celery. Cook for about 5 minutes or until the vegetables are soft.

2. Add in the garlic, thyme, parsley, and smoked paprika and sauté 1 minute longer.

3. Stir in the chicken broth, bay leaves, and cooked chorizo. If your chorizo isn't spicy (or if you like more spice), this is a good time to add a pinch of red pepper flakes to the pot. Let the soup simmer for about 15 minutes.

4. Stir in the beans, keeping the heat on low. Let the stew gently simmer for about 10 more minutes to allow the flavors to develop. Stir in the white wine vinegar and then season with salt and pepper to taste.

5. This stew gets better with time. If I have the time, I let it simmer on low for about 1 hour, adding more broth if necessary. Then I remove it from the heat and let it rest for another 10 minutes.

6. Serve warm. This stew will keep in the refrigerator for several days.

Note: Soy chorizo can also be used here, but it won't need to be cooked. Just slice and brown and add it to the stew. This makes a nice vegetarian substitute.

NEHALEM RIVER RANCH

JARED GARDNER / NEHALEM, OREGON

Nehalem River Ranch is a 100-acre farm on the stunning north Oregon coast, home to pasture-raised cattle and pigs. It's nestled in a valley bordered to the north and south by the Tillamook State Forest, and on the southern edge of the pastures flows the beautiful Nehalem River.

Jared Gardner is the owner/rancher of Nehalem River Ranch, which has earned the prestigious Certified AWA (Animal Welfare Approved by A Greener World) and is an AGA-certified (American Grassfed Association) producer. Jared raises his cattle and pigs on nutrient-dense pastures with a holistic planned grazing system. This holistic system ensures a healthy environment for the animals and encourages their natural behavior by providing a tranquil environment. Jared says, "Pigs are able to frolic and root, and cows meander and graze together."

Nehalem River Ranch beef is proudly featured by talented local chefs on the coast and in Portland. At the end of every September, the ranch hosts an annual Argentine asado, a style of open-fire barbecue that is typically a 3-day event. Jared was inspired to begin this delicious tradition at Nehalem River Ranch after spending time in Argentina and with the Argentine

community in Portland. His approach to raising grass-fed cattle was a direct result of time spent at these community asados. It's a celebration of family, friends, and community cooking—a large meal outdoors, savoring Mother Earth and her landscape while sharing the delicious food.

During one of the community asado celebrations at the ranch, Jared wrote a passage that sums up his love and passion for life on his Oregon ranch: "Some days the sun gently warms the pastures and the bugs hum, and the barn swallows chase each other around the sky. And every day I journey between my house, the barns, and the cattle pastures, evaluating the grass, planning the rotations. I pass the beehives in the eastern pasture near the willows and then I pass vegetable fields and I'm struck by how beautiful this place is. How lucky we are to live here and be in life with this community."

Chicken and Rosemary Lemon Dumplings

SERVES 4

I like to think of this recipe as a warm, cozy blanket in a bowl. It's a cheerful winter dish brimming with herb and citrus flavors, making this the perfect meal for cold weather months.

I like to use chicken thighs in this recipe due to their rich flavor and higher fat content. The chicken thigh meat gives a depth of flavor that you won't get with chicken breasts. However, if chicken breasts are your preference, this recipe will still be delicious. Be careful not to overcook the chicken breasts, as they will get tough and chewy.

For the Soup

2 tablespoons ghee, extra virgin olive oil, or avocado oil, plus more as needed

8 boneless, skinless chicken thighs (about 2 pounds)

Salt and pepper, to taste

1 yellow onion, diced

2 carrots, diced

1 rib celery, diced

3 cloves garlic, minced

1 tablespoon chopped fresh parsley

1 tablespoon chopped fresh chives

½ teaspoon dried thyme

¼ cup all-purpose flour

4 cups chicken broth

For the Dumplings

1 cup all-purpose flour

2 teaspoons baking powder

½ teaspoon salt

2 teaspoons finely chopped fresh rosemary

Zest of 1 lemon (about 1 teaspoon)

1 egg

¼ cup milk plus more as needed

Chopped fresh chives, for garnish

1. To make the soup: In a Dutch oven or heavy-bottomed pot, heat the ghee over medium-high heat. Season the chicken thighs with salt and pepper.

2. When the ghee is hot, brown the chicken thighs. You may need to do this in batches, as loading the pot will decrease the temperature and the chicken may not brown properly.

3. Transfer the browned chicken thighs to a plate and reserve.

4. Add additional ghee to the pot if needed, and then add the onion, carrots, and celery and sauté until the vegetables are softened and onions are translucent, 5 to 8 minutes. Stir in the garlic, parsley, chives, and thyme and cook for 1 minute longer.

5. Stir in the flour and continue stirring for about 30 seconds to 1 minute. Stir in the chicken broth and bring it to a boil. Once it reaches a boil, turn down the heat to a low simmer.

6. Cube the browned chicken into bite-size pieces and add the chicken and any drippings back into the pot with the broth and vegetables. Let the mixture simmer on low while you prepare the dumplings. Season to taste with salt and pepper.

7. To make the dumplings: In a medium bowl, add the flour, baking powder, salt, rosemary, and lemon zest. Mix to combine. Mix in the egg and the milk. You may need an additional tablespoon or more of milk in order to achieve a somewhat sticky dough.

8. With a muffin scoop or a tablespoon, drop dumplings gently into the simmering chicken and vegetable mixture. Try to evenly space the dumplings when dropping them into the pot. They will expand as they cook.

9. Cover with a lid and simmer on low for about 10 minutes, letting the dumplings steam. The dumplings should be puffed up a bit and covering the top

of the soup. If you like a little color on your dumplings or a bit of a toasty top, turn the oven on broil and place your Dutch oven or large pot in the oven, allowing the top of the dumplings to brown.

10. Ladle into bowls, garnish with chopped fresh chives, and serve.

Roasted Garlic and Dungeness Crab Soup

RECIPE FROM LOCAL OCEAN SEAFOOD IN NEWPORT, OREGON

SERVES 8

I order this drool-worthy soup every time we dine at Local Ocean Seafood. It's creamy, garlicky, loaded with flavor, and filled with the freshest crab. Now that I have the recipe, I also make it in my home kitchen on special occasions, especially when crab season opens for the year.

Thank you, Local Ocean Seafood, for sharing your house soup recipe.

3 large heads garlic

4 tablespoons olive oil

1 tablespoon plus 1 teaspoon minced shallot

1 tablespoon plus 1 teaspoon minced green onion

4 tablespoons (½ stick) unsalted butter

¼ cup rice flour or ½ cup all-purpose flour (see notes)

8¼ cups water

1 tablespoon clam base (see notes)

1¾ teaspoons lobster base (see notes)

¼ cup dry white wine

1½ cups half-and-half or heavy cream

½ cup grated Parmesan, plus more for serving

Salt, to taste

1 pound fresh crab meat, picked over to remove shells and cartilage

Fennel sprigs, for garnish

1. Preheat the oven to 400°F.

2. Pull the papery outer layers from the garlic heads and trim the top ½ inch off each head. Place the heads on a large sheet of aluminum foil, drizzle with 1 tablespoon of the olive oil, and wrap tightly in the foil. Roast for about 1 hour or until the garlic is soft in the center. Let cool and then squeeze the roasted garlic out of each clove. Measure out ½ cup of roasted garlic and set aside.

3. Place the remaining garlic in a mini food processor or blender and add 3 tablespoons of the olive oil with the shallot and green onion. Blend until a paste forms and set aside.

4. Make a roux by melting the butter in a small saucepan and whisking in the flour until smooth. Cook, stirring constantly, for 2 to 3 minutes. Remove from heat and set aside.

5. In a large stockpot, combine the water, clam base, and lobster base. Bring to a boil, reduce heat, and add the white wine, reserved ½ cup roasted garlic, and half-and-half. Simmer for 5 minutes and then whisk in the roux and ½ cup Parmesan. Return to a simmer and continue simmering for 30 to 45 minutes or until reduced to 6 or 7 cups. Taste and add salt if desired.

6. To serve, divide the crab among 8 soup bowls, top each with a large pinch of Parmesan and 1½ teaspoons of the garlic-shallot paste. Pour ¾ cup of hot soup into each bowl and top with a sprig of fennel. Serve immediately.

Notes: Rice flour is available everywhere (Bob's Red Mill is a popular brand), but if you would prefer to buy a small amount, look for it in the bulk foods section.

This recipe was tested using Better Than Bouillon brand clam and lobster bases, which are available at most markets and online.

LOCAL OCEAN SEAFOOD

CHEF ENRIQUE SANCHEZ / NEWPORT, OREGON

On Newport, Oregon's historic waterfront, you'll find one of the best restaurants on the coast, Local Ocean Seafood. The creative force behind the food at Local Ocean Seafood is Executive Chef Enrique Sanchez.

Chef Enrique grew up in south Mexico City in a small village in the state of Puebla. His love of cooking was inspired by his mother and grandmother. They could often be found cooking a large meal of pork and a fresh tomato and green bean stew over an open fire for their weekly family gatherings.

Those family gatherings and a love for fresh, local food are Chef Enrique's inspirations when creating new dishes for the Local Ocean Seafood menu. He uses a diverse selection of fresh, seasonal ingredients to design delicious combinations of flavors for the palate, as well as pure beauty on the plate. And what's not to love with flavor combinations such as grilled halibut with poblano peppers, mozzarella, and fresh summer peaches? Or a succulent crab po'boy sandwich filled with a green chili avocado puree and topped with a butter-soft bun?

Given all the mouthwatering dishes on the menu, it's no surprise that Local Ocean Seafood and Chef Enrique have won numerous culinary awards over

the years. Although the exquisite menu takes center stage, Local Ocean Seafood also has an inviting ambiance that makes me want to hang around for hours while grazing through the entire menu.

During our interview, I asked Chef Enrique what inspires him to create a recipe. He responded with: "Colleagues, moments, places, ingredients... but, most of all, the customers who come to dine at the restaurant. The patrons' thanks and compliments and the joy the food brings to them is one of my greatest inspirations." He added, "One has to feel the passion to create the food. When the customer is having a great experience and enjoying the food, that is the goal; I am inspired."

Northwest-Style Smoked Salmon Chowder

SERVES 4

You know you're from the Pacific Northwest when, every time you dine at a restaurant, you rate the chowder. My daughters grew up here, and yes, they rate the chowder at every restaurant, which always makes me laugh. For my two gals, a chowder can be passable or good, really good but not perfect, or perfect. Their perfect chowder has just the right amount of creaminess, is seasoned well, and is nicely loaded with potatoes and seafood.

This Northwest-Style Smoked Salmon Chowder is the chowder recipe I make most often at home and it happens to get a "perfect" rating from my two chowder judges. This recipe combines the slight sweetness of leeks, the creamy texture of potatoes, and the distinctive flavor of fresh dill. It's finished with a little heavy cream and a hint of allspice.

Because it doesn't sit long on the stovetop, I've added a teaspoon of rice wine vinegar at the end. This simply brings all the flavors together quickly. I like to serve this dish with my Savory Beer Bread with Garlic, Cheddar, and Fresh Herbs (page 28).

3 tablespoons unsalted butter

1 large leek or 2 small leeks, finely diced (white and light green parts only)

3 cloves garlic, minced

1 medium carrot, diced small

1½ pounds potatoes, cut into bite-size pieces

2 to 3 cups vegetable or chicken broth, enough to cover the potatoes

½ teaspoon allspice

1 dried bay leaf

1 cup heavy cream

10 to 12 ounces smoked salmon, shredded or diced (not lox)

Salt and black pepper, to taste

1 tablespoon cornstarch mixed with 1 tablespoon cold water (optional)

1 bunch fresh dill, chopped

1 teaspoon rice wine or white wine vinegar

1. In a soup pot over medium heat, add the butter. When the butter has melted, add the leeks and cook until they are soft and wilted.

2. Stir in the garlic and carrot and cook 1 minute longer. Add the potatoes, broth, allspice, and bay leaf. Bring the liquid to a boil and then turn down the heat to a simmer. Let the soup simmer for about 15 minutes, or until the potatoes are soft.

3. Once the potatoes are soft, use a wooden spoon or potato masher to mash about half the potatoes. This will create a creamy, thicker texture. Stir in the heavy cream and smoked salmon. Bring to a lively simmer for 1 to 2 minutes and then take it off the heat. Season to taste with salt and pepper.

4. If you'd like a thicker chowder, mix together the cornstarch and cold water. Turn the heat to medium and, while the chowder is simmering, stir in the slurry (cornstarch and water). As the chowder simmers, the slurry will thicken the texture.

5. Take the soup pot off the heat and stir in the chopped fresh dill and vinegar. Let the soup sit for 5 to 10 minutes, then serve.

NEWPORT FISHERMEN'S WIVES

NEWPORT, OREGON

Newport is a small seaside town located on the mid-Oregon coast. With stunning views of the Pacific Ocean and a shoreline dotted with tide pools and sea life, Newport is home to historical landmarks, lighthouses, and one of Oregon's largest fishing fleets. It's also where I found an exceptional group of trailblazing women called the Newport Fishermen's Wives.

This group of innovative women was formed in 1970 by several local fishermen's wives. The organization is a non-profit corporation and consists of fishermen's wives, mothers, daughters, and friends who support the seaside community to further the causes of industry, safety, seafood education, and family support.

I had the pleasure of meeting a few of the current members and executive board one sunny spring afternoon on the coast. As we dined on the most delicious seafood, most likely caught that very morning,

Taunette Dixon, president of the Newport Fishermen's Wives, shared the history and current role of this important organization.

Life in a fishing community can be challenging and, through the hard work and efforts of the Newport Fishermen's Wives, they are able to provide much-needed assistance to fishing families, fund scholarships for local students, coordinate an annual holiday outreach program, and sponsor local events such as the annual blessing of the fleet. Most recently, the Newport Fishermen's Wives fought a long federal court battle to save Newport's rescue helicopter. Because of their action, today the ocean waters off the Oregon coast are safer, not only for the commercial fishing fleet but the recreational fishing fleet as well.

There is no doubt that when a need arises, or tragedy strikes, the Newport Fishermen's Wives step in and meet the challenge of supporting this unique seaside community.

Pacific Northwest–Style Fishermen's Stew

SERVES 6 TO 8

This recipe is much like the Italian dish cioppino: a fish stew with a hearty tomato base. It has a rich broth filled with fresh herbs and a variety of local Oregon shellfish and fish. I serve this hearty recipe with warm crusty bread for dipping in the flavorful broth. If you can't find all the seafood I've listed in the recipe, feel free to substitute with what you have available. I think white fish, shrimp, and either mussels or clams always make a nice combination.

2 tablespoons extra virgin olive oil

1 red onion, diced

1 medium red pepper, diced

1 small fennel bulb, diced

3 cloves garlic, minced

¼ cup chopped Italian parsley leaves, plus 1 tablespoon for garnish

1 teaspoon chopped fresh oregano

3 sprigs fresh thyme

½ teaspoon crushed red pepper flakes

1 teaspoon smoked paprika

2 cups red wine such as Pinot Noir or other light and dry varietal

One 15-ounce can tomato sauce

2 to 4 cups seafood stock, vegetable stock, or chicken broth

Salt and pepper, to taste

1 pound fresh mussels, cleaned

1 pound fresh clams, cleaned

½ pound Oregon or small bay shrimp

8 ounces fresh Dungeness crabmeat (optional)

1 pound halibut or Pacific cod, cubed

Shaved Parmesan, for garnish

1 sourdough baguette, warmed and sliced, to serve

1. In a large pot or Dutch oven, heat the oil over medium heat. When the oil is hot, add onion, red pepper, and fennel. When the aromatics are soft and wilted, add garlic, Italian parsley, oregano, sprigs of thyme, red pepper flakes, and smoked paprika. Let this cook for about 1 minute.

2. Stir in red wine and reduce by half. Then turn down the heat and stir in the tomato sauce. Bring the liquid to a simmer and let it cook on low for about 10 minutes.

3. Stir in 2 cups of seafood stock (or vegetable stock or chicken broth). Season to taste with salt and pepper.

4. Add the mussels and clams, cover the pot, and simmer until the shellfish have opened their shells and the meat is cooked, 5 to 8 minutes.

5. Add in the shrimp and Dungeness crab, if using, and halibut or cod. Add more stock or broth to the stew if needed. It should have the consistency of a stew, not a soup.

6. Heat until the liquid is simmering and then remove from heat. Let it sit covered for about 10 minutes. Season to taste with salt and pepper.

7. To serve, ladle stew in bowls and garnish with chopped Italian parsley and shaved Parmesan. Serve with slices of warm and crusty sourdough baguette.

Cowgirl Chili with Winter Squash

SERVES 6

When my youngest daughter was 4 years old, she asked me why our chili recipe was called Cowboy Chili. As I was trying to answer her question, she proceeded to inform me there were no cowboys in our house and she felt the recipe should be called Cowgirl Chili. This made me smile, because at that moment, I realized my daughter was going to take life by the reins and lead it where she desires.

This Cowgirl Chili with Winter Squash is my house chili recipe that I prepare with Martson Farm ground beef, a variety of spices, beans, a bottle of local beer, and winter squash. The beer is used for enhanced flavor and the alcohol is eliminated during cooking. But if you would rather not use beer in this chili, 12 ounces of beef broth is a nice substitute. When I serve the chili, I set out bowls of sour cream, Cheddar, cilantro, and green onions for garnishes.

2 tablespoons masa or corn flour (don't use cornmeal)—or mix 2 teaspoons cornstarch with 2 teaspoons cold water to make a slurry to add at the end of cooking instead

½ teaspoon cinnamon

1 teaspoon smoked paprika

1 tablespoon chili powder

1 teaspoon ground coriander

1 teaspoon ground cumin

1 tablespoon brown sugar

Pinch of cayenne (optional)

4 tablespoons avocado oil or ghee

1 large yellow onion, chopped

3 to 4 cloves garlic, minced

1 pound ground beef

1 tablespoon tomato paste

One 12-ounce bottle beer (pilsner or lager; red ale or cream stout is also good)

2 to 3 pounds winter squash, about 2 cups bite-size cubes (I use butternut or delicata)

One 15-ounce can black beans, with liquid

One 15-ounce can kidney beans or chili beans, with liquid

1 dried bay leaf

1 to 2 cups beef broth, if needed

Salt and pepper, to taste

1 tablespoon of lime juice

Sour cream, Cheddar, chopped cilantro, and green onions, for garnish

1. In a small bowl, mix together the masa, cinnamon, smoked paprika, chili powder, coriander, cumin, and brown sugar. (If you opt to make the cornstarch slurry instead of using masa, you'll add it in at the end of cooking to thicken the chili; see step 5.) Add the cayenne, if using.

2. In a large pot over medium-high heat, add 2 tablespoons oil. Once the oil is hot, add the onion and sauté just until it's tender. Add the garlic and ground beef. While you're cooking the ground beef, stir in the masa-spice mixture.

3. Once the ground beef is mostly cooked, add the tomato paste, beer, and squash. Stir until incorporated. Once the chili has come to a boil, turn the heat down to medium-low and add both cans of beans, bay leaf, and at least 1 cup of broth. Reserve the remaining broth and use it as needed.

4. Let the chili simmer on low for 25 to 30 minutes, or until the squash is tender. Season to taste with salt and pepper, and stir in a squeeze of lime.

5. If using the cornstarch slurry to thicken the chili, turn the heat to medium high and stir in the slurry. Let the chili simmer for 1 to 2 minutes to thicken. Take the chili off the heat and let it cool for 10 minutes prior to serving.

6. Serve with sour cream, Cheddar, cilantro, and green onion, if desired. This chili will keep for 3 to 4 days in the refrigerator.

MARTSON FARM

RICK MARTSON / MOLALLA, OREGON

How does a trial lawyer end up becoming a Scottish Highland cattle farmer? Certainly not without a passion for farming, and Rick Martson has a genuine enthusiasm for raising Highland cattle. He grew up in Pennsylvania, where his love of farming developed while working regularly on local farms as well as his aunt and uncle's farm. After spending a year in Edinburgh, Scotland, for undergraduate studies, he met his first wife, Debbie. They eventually moved to Molalla, Oregon, and bought Bagby Homestead, a 100-year-old farm, in 1974.

Over the next 30 years, Martson Farm became a labor of love for Rick. Even during the height of his law career, he always found time to work on his farm. This commitment to pasture-raising Scottish Highland cattle led to growing the farm to nearly 300 acres. The farm is a stunning palette of lush pasture and hillside forest, ideal for naturally raising the oldest registered breed of cattle.

Martson Farm's 160 head of Scottish Highland cattle are only grass fed and finished, and they graze naturally for up to three full years, which is one year longer than traditional breeds of cattle. The beef is lower in fat and cholesterol and it has a rich flavor and succulent texture, making it an exquisite choice for pretty much any recipe.

My visit to Martson Farm included a wander through the pastures snapping photos of the calves and a very interesting conversation with Rick about life on the farm. Rick and his lovely wife, Susan, were gracious hosts, and the visit left me with a deep appreciation and respect for a life committed to raising the best quality food possible for our community.

You can find Martson Farm Highland beef on the farm's website (they deliver within 50 miles) and it can also be purchased from their booth at the Silverton Farmers' Market in Silverton, Oregon.

Corn and Roasted Poblano Chowder

SERVES 4 TO 6

We are fortunate to have a large selection of farmers' markets in Oregon. I make it my mission to visit as many as possible during the summer months. They're all a little different and I never know what I might find.

I am notorious for walking these farmers' markets and buying more produce than I can use. For me, it's like being a kid in a candy store. So when I've purchased more sweet corn than I really need and a few pounds of shiny green poblano peppers, this chowder recipe happens.

I think this recipe tastes best with fresh corn from the cob, but when fresh corn isn't available, I like to use frozen sweet corn. Roasting the poblano peppers prior to adding them to the chowder gives the soup a rich, deep, and smoky flavor that complements the sweetness of the corn. The rice wine vinegar adds a smidgen of acidity that brings all the flavors together. I find that quick soups—that is, soups that don't simmer for long periods of time—need a little boost. Rice wine vinegar or white wine vinegar works well in chowders such as this one.

½ pound bacon, chopped

2 tablespoons unsalted butter

1 large yellow onion, diced

2 cloves garlic, minced

Two 3-inch sprigs fresh thyme

1 tablespoon chopped fresh parsley

3 poblano peppers, roasted, seeded, and diced

1½ pounds red or yellow potatoes, cubed into bite-size pieces

2 to 3 cups vegetable or chicken broth

2 cups fresh or frozen corn

½ to 1 cup heavy cream

Salt and pepper, to taste

1 teaspoon rice wine vinegar

1 tablespoon cornstarch mixed with 1 tablespoon cold water (optional)

Sliced green onions and shredded Cheddar or Swiss cheese, for garnish

1. In a large soup pot over medium heat, add the chopped bacon and cook until the bacon is slightly crispy and the fat is rendered, meaning the fat from the bacon has melted into the pan. Transfer the bacon to a bowl and transfer all the rendered bacon fat to a jar. Then add 1 tablespoon of bacon fat back to the soup pot.

2. With the soup pot over medium heat, add the butter to the 1 tablespoon bacon fat. Stir in the onion and cook until soft and slightly golden. Stir in the garlic and cook 1 minute longer.

3. Add the fresh thyme, parsley, diced poblano peppers, potatoes, and 2 cups broth. You want enough broth to cover the potatoes. Bring the soup to a boil, turn down the heat to low, and simmer for 15 to 20 minutes, or until the potatoes are soft.

4. Stir in the corn, reserved bacon, and heavy cream and bring the soup back to a simmer. Season to taste with salt and pepper.

5. Add the rice wine vinegar.

6. If you prefer a thicker chowder, add the slurry of cornstarch and water to the chowder while the chowder is simmering. Let it simmer for at least 1 to 2 minutes to thicken.

7. Once the chowder is done, ladle it into bowls and garnish with sliced green onions and shredded Cheddar or Swiss cheese.

Summer Harvest Gazpacho

SERVES 4

Gazpacho is the perfect summer soup and it's a delicious way to use fresh summer Oregon tomatoes. I've also added roasted red pepper and smoked paprika to this recipe, which creates a slightly richer flavor and balances nicely with the cucumber. It's a bright and colorful soup and makes a gorgeous starter for a summer barbecue.

2 pounds fresh summer tomatoes, sliced in half

2 medium to large cloves garlic

1 medium cucumber, peeled, seeded, and chopped, plus more diced for garnish

1 medium red bell pepper, roasted, skinned, and seeded

1 jalapeño, seeded

1 tablespoon chopped parsley

¼ cup basil leaves

½ cup chopped red onion

1 teaspoon smoked paprika

1 teaspoon granulated sugar

1 teaspoon salt, plus more to taste

½ teaspoon pepper, plus more to taste

2 tablespoons sherry vinegar

1 cup diced stale bread

¼ cup good quality extra virgin olive oil

Homemade croutons, for garnish

1. Add the tomatoes, garlic, cucumber, red pepper, jalapeño, parsley, basil, onion, smoked paprika, sugar, salt, pepper, and sherry vinegar to a blender or food processor. Pulse or blend on low until the ingredients are pureed but there is still some texture to the soup.

2. Add the stale bread and extra virgin olive oil. Puree just until the soup is nicely combined. Add salt and pepper to taste.

3. Serve slightly chilled or at room temperature. Ladle soup into bowls and garnish with homemade croutons and additional diced fresh cucumber. You can make this soup in advance and hold it in the refrigerator for up to 2 days.

Note: To make croutons, preheat the oven to 375°F. Add 2 to 3 cups day-old or stale bread cubes to a large bowl and toss with ¼ cup extra virgin olive oil and ½ teaspoon salt. Spread the bread cubes on a baking sheet, place in the oven. Bake for about 5 minutes. If they haven't browned up enough, leave them in the oven another 3 to 5 minutes. Remove the croutons from the oven and let them cool. Store in an airtight container for up to 1 week.

COWHORN VINEYARD & GARDEN

BARBARA AND BILL STEELE / JACKSONVILLE, OREGON

Early one June morning, I met Cowhorn Vineyard & Garden cofounder and winemaker Bill Steele at his enchanting estate vineyard, which is tucked away in the historic Applegate Valley in southern Oregon.

After prestigious careers on Wall Street and in finance, Bill and Barbara Steele decided to leave the Bay Area and move north to pursue their passion for organic, sustainable farming in southern Oregon. Together, they started Cowhorn Vineyard & Garden and now grow and produce wines exclusively from the Cowhorn estate vineyard.

The 117-acre polyculture farm sits along the pristine Applegate River. The farm is skirted by old-growth forests and nestled on valley land rich in minerals. It is a favorable environment for growing classic Rhône grape varietals such as Syrah, Grenache, Viognier, Marsanne, and Roussanne. In addition to growing grape varietals, Cowhorn also grows asparagus, lavender, and hazelnuts.

This exquisite boutique vineyard has earned numerous wine accolades over the past 11 years. It's also the first winery tasting room in the United States to meet the zero-energy, toxin-free Living Building Challenge. Bill and Barbara Steele have spent the last 15 years working to create an organic and certified biodynamic farm, vineyard, and winery that works to support the surrounding ecosystem. Today, more than half the estate is reserved for habitat, forest, and riparian areas.

As I walked Cowhorn Vineyard & Garden while listening to Bill and Barbara's captivating story, I was reminded of the quote by Spanish writer Pedro Calderón de la Barca: "Green is the prime color of the world, and that from which its loveliness arises." Cowhorn Vineyard & Garden is truly a place from which loveliness and great wine arises.

Black Bean Soup with Griddle Cakes

SERVES 4

Black Bean Soup with Griddle Cakes is my answer to serving a healthy soup with a side of comfort. In addition to black beans, I've added aromatics, herbs, smoked paprika, and locally sourced bacon. These ingredients enhance the flavor and texture of the black beans and make the most delightful meal when served with little griddle cakes.

For the Soup

1 tablespoon avocado oil or extra virgin olive oil

4 ounces bacon, diced

1 small white onion, diced

1 medium carrot, diced

3 cloves garlic, minced

Two 15-ounce cans organic black beans, drained

1 teaspoon smoked paprika

½ teaspoon black pepper

½ teaspoon dried oregano

1 tablespoon chopped fresh parsley

1 heaping tablespoon tomato paste

2 to 3 cups vegetable or chicken broth

Juice of half a lime

Salt and pepper, to taste

Sprigs of fresh cilantro and lime wedges, for garnish

Sour cream or dairy-free sour cream, to serve

For the Griddle Cakes

½ cup all-purpose flour

1 cup finely ground cornmeal

1 teaspoon granulated sugar

1 teaspoon baking powder

1 teaspoon salt

1 egg, lightly beaten

¾ to 1 cup hot whole milk

1 tablespoon extra virgin olive oil or ghee

Butter and honey, to serve

1. Place a soup pot over medium heat and add the oil. When the oil is hot, add the bacon. When the bacon is crisp, remove it from the pot with a slotted spoon, leaving at least one tablespoon of the rendered fat.

2. Add the onion and carrot. Sauté over medium-low heat and let the veggies sweat for 3 to 5 minutes. When the onions are soft, add the garlic. Sauté for about 1 minute longer.

3. Stir in the black beans, smoked paprika, black pepper, oregano, parsley, tomato paste, and 2 cups broth. Bring the soup to a slow boil, then turn the heat down to a simmer for about 15 minutes. Add additional broth for a thinner soup.

4. While the soup is simmering, make the griddle cakes. In an electric mixer or large bowl, combine the flour, cornmeal, sugar, baking powder, and salt. As you whisk, add the egg, ¾ cup hot milk, and olive oil. Add the remaining milk if you need to thin the batter.

5. Heat a griddle pan or skillet over medium-low heat and drop tablespoon-size dollops of batter onto the pan. These are cooked just like a pancake, so when the batter is a little bubbly in the center, flip the griddle cake to the other side. When they're done, place the griddle cakes on a platter to cool. Serve the griddle cakes with butter and honey.

6. To finish the soup, stir in the lime juice and season to taste with salt and pepper. Serve in bowls with fresh cilantro, lime wedges, sour cream, or dairy-free sour cream and the griddle cakes.

SALADS, SIDES, AND VEGETABLES

Shaved Brussels Sprouts Salad with Winter Squash, Dried Cherries, and Bacon with Maple Vinaigrette

SERVES 4 TO 6

I always think the ingredients in this salad represent the variety of beautiful ingredients from an Oregon harvest. The salad's base is made of thinly shaved fresh Brussels sprouts, which are then combined with roasted winter squash, dried cherries, crispy bacon, and Oregon hazelnuts, all tossed in the most delicious maple vinaigrette.

The colors in this salad look quite festive on the dinner table and, although I serve this as a side salad for Sunday dinner, it can certainly be served à la carte as an entrée salad.

For the Vinaigrette

½ cup extra virgin olive oil

3 tablespoons apple cider vinegar

3 tablespoons maple syrup (or to taste)

1 tablespoon Dijon mustard

1 clove garlic, minced

Salt and freshly cracked black pepper, to taste

For the Salad

1 pound organic Brussels sprouts, shaved with a
    mandolin or sliced thin with a knife

4 ounces cooked bacon, diced

1 cup diced roasted winter squash or sweet potato
    (I often use delicata squash for their sweet,
    nutty flavor)

2 tablespoons finely chopped green onion

½ cup dried cherries (or cranberries)

½ cup toasted hazelnuts, chopped

Salt and pepper, to taste

3 ounces crumbled goat cheese,
    for garnish (optional)

Handful of microgreens, chopped (optional)

1. To make the vinaigrette: In a small bowl, whisk together the olive oil, apple cider vinegar, maple syrup, mustard, and garlic. Season to taste with salt and pepper.

2. To make the salad: In a large bowl, gently toss together the shaved Brussels sprouts, diced bacon, winter squash, green onion, dried cherries, and hazelnuts.

3. You can keep this salad covered in the refrigerator for about 2 hours. Just before serving, toss gently with dressing to taste (reserving additional dressing if needed) and season with salt and pepper. Pour out onto a platter or into a large bowl and garnish with crumbled goat cheese and microgreens, if using. Serve immediately.

LUCKY CROW FARM

EDEN OLSEN / MONMOUTH, OREGON

Eden Olsen's love of growing vegetables was cultivated by her mother, who grew much of what their family ate. Her mom started multiple community gardens in their hometown, one of which has now become part of Lucky Crow Farm. Eden's father grew up on a local grass seed farm. One could say that farming runs in the family.

After studying sustainable agriculture and food policy in college, Eden went on to manage farmers' markets in the Bay Area and worked on several farms in California and Washington. Eventually, Eden returned home and started her own operation, Lucky Crow Farm, growing healthy sustainable food for her neighbors.

Eden says, "Farming marries my passion and logic, creating a beautiful and sometimes absurd love-child." She farms because she

believes that access to healthy food is a basic human right, and she intends to feed delicious, nutrient-rich food to the diverse local community throughout the seasons.

Lucky Crow Farm began in 2017 and has now flourished into three urban locations, which meant hiring farm manager Ash Sigl. Eden strives to hire women and support female-owned businesses because she knows that the future must be rooted in equality. I think the Lucky Crow Farm slogan says it all: "Female-powered, minimal till, grown with love."

You can find Eden, Ash, and Lucky Crow Farm produce at the Saturday Corvallis Farmers' Market. Or check them out online for more information about their CSA (community supported agriculture) program.

Roasted Winter Beet Salad with Candied Nuts and Blue Cheese

SERVES 4 TO 6

It took me a long time to like beets. I used to get them in my local CSA (community supported agriculture) box, much like the beautiful boxes of produce from our local Lucky Crow Farm, and I ended up grating them into salads, pickling, or juicing them. But it wasn't until I started roasting them that I truly fell in love with this jewel-colored root vegetable.

In this recipe, the beets are roasted, sliced, and layered on a platter. I scatter a bit of marinated shallots, candied nuts, and blue cheese over the top and drizzle with a balsamic reduction and my best extra virgin olive oil. This recipe makes a lovely warm salad for a cool fall or winter evening.

6 medium red or gold beets (or a mixture of both)

¼ cup plus 1 tablespoon extra virgin olive oil

2 medium shallots, peeled and thinly sliced

½ cup good quality balsamic vinegar

Salt and pepper, to taste

4 ounces crumbled blue cheese or gorgonzola

½ cup chopped candied hazelnuts, walnuts, or pecans

1. Preheat the oven to 400°F.

2. Wash the beets and trim them up a bit. Toss them with 1 tablespoon of the olive oil. Place them in the center of a large piece of aluminum foil and wrap them, tenting the foil a little so they have room to steam. Place them on a baking sheet and roast the beets for about 45 minutes or until the beets are fork tender.

3. Remove the beets from the oven and let them cool completely.

4. While the beets are roasting, add the sliced shallots to a non-reactive bowl and toss them with 2 tablespoons of the balsamic vinegar. Let them rest in the vinegar for about 30 minutes. You can also make these 1 day in advance and keep them refrigerated.

5. In a small saucepan, add the remaining balsamic vinegar and, over medium heat, bring the vinegar to a simmer. Turn the heat to low. Simmer just until the vinegar has reduced by half and it has a syrupy texture. Take it off the heat and keep warm.

6. When the beets are cool, slice them and layer them on a platter. Sprinkle with a little salt and pepper. Layer the marinated shallots over the beets and drizzle the beets with the warm balsamic reduction. Then drizzle with ¼ cup extra virgin olive oil, and top with the crumbled cheese and candied nuts. Serve immediately.

Note: To make candied nuts, mix together 1 cup chopped nuts, 1 tablespoon unsalted butter, and ¼ cup sugar in a nonstick pan over medium heat for about 5 minutes, stirring constantly. The sugar will begin to melt and coat the nuts. Once the nuts are coated, transfer them to wax paper in a single layer and let them cool. Break them apart as needed and use them on salads or as a snack.

Layered Cornbread Salad with Spicy Avocado Ranch Dressing

SERVES 6 TO 8

Layered salads were all the rage where I grew up, and they were front and center on every potluck table. I especially enjoyed the layered salads that included cornbread. The memory of these salads and all our locally grown produce inspired me to create this recipe for our large dinner or barbecue gatherings—which usually involves several hungry college students.

I like to serve this salad in a trifle bowl. The layers are bright in color and the salad makes a pretty presentation on the table. If you don't have a clear glass trifle bowl, any deep salad bowl will do.

For the Dressing

1 large avocado

Juice of 1 lime

1 cup mayonnaise

½ to ¾ cup buttermilk

1 chipotle pepper in adobo

1 packet ranch dressing seasoning mix

½ cup water as needed

For the Salad

3 to 4 cups shredded iceberg lettuce, romaine lettuce, or cabbage (or a mixture of all three)

Salt, to taste

1 cup crumbled cornbread (you can also sub with coarsely crushed tortilla chips)

1 pint cherry tomatoes, halved

1 to 2 avocados, diced

½ cup diced red onions

One 15-ounce can black beans, rinsed and drained

½ cup sliced green onions

One 15-ounce can corn, drained, or 1½ cups cooked and cooled corn

1 bunch cilantro, coarsely chopped

½ cup crumbled cotija cheese

Sliced green onions, for garnish

1. In a food processor or blender, make the dressing by adding the avocado, lime juice, mayonnaise, buttermilk, chipotle pepper, and ranch dressing seasoning mix. Pulse until thoroughly combined and smooth. If needed, add a few tablespoons of water to thin the dressing. This should make 2 cups of dressing.

2. To assemble the salad: Add lettuce to the bottom of a glass salad or trifle bowl. Lightly sprinkle with salt. Sprinkle the cornbread or tortilla crumbles over the lettuce. Top with half the dressing.

3. Cover the cornbread and dressing with the tomatoes, then the avocados, next the red onions, black beans, green onions, and corn. Then top the corn with the cilantro, then the cotija cheese, and garnish with green onions.

4. Chill the salad until ready to serve. Serve with a side of the remaining dressing.

Note: Feel free to sub or add additional fresh ingredients such as chopped red, yellow, or green peppers, chopped poblano, pepper Jack cheese, etc.

Blackberry Burrata Salad

SERVES 4

One of the best things about hot summer weather is fresh Oregon blackberries. We have a plethora of berries here, but blackberries make summer in Oregon delicious. I use blackberries in everything from breakfast recipes to savory fish recipes, desserts, and salads to sauces.

Berries almost always pair deliciously with cheese and our prized Oregon wine, so I've paired a creamy burrata with blackberries in this beautiful summer salad, and serve it with a crisp Oregon Pinot Gris.

For the Dressing

½ cup extra virgin olive oil

3 tablespoons balsamic vinegar

2 tablespoons honey

1 tablespoon Dijon mustard

Dash of water

Salt and pepper, to taste

For the Salad

6 to 8 ounces assorted baby salad greens

½ pint heirloom cherry tomatoes, halved

1 pint fresh blackberries

1 to 2 knobs burrata cheese, sliced right before serving the salad

Fresh small basil leaves, for garnish

Pinch of gourmet finishing salt, for garnish (optional)

1. Whisk together the olive oil, balsamic vinegar, honey, mustard, and dash of water. Season to taste with salt and pepper.

2. In a large bowl, add the salad greens and lightly dress with the vinaigrette. Layer four salad plates with salad greens and then top with halved cherry tomatoes, blackberries, and slices of burrata cheese. Garnish with fresh small basil leaves and finishing salt, if using. Serve the salads with additional dressing on the side.

Mexican Corn and Tomato Salad

SERVES 4 TO 6

My family loves elote, which is grilled Mexican street corn. We make elote all summer long with fresh Oregon corn from our local farms. However, as much as I love corn prepared this way, I thought it would be just as fun and delicious in salad form.

To make the salad a bit more hearty, I've added tomatoes and red onions. I've kept the elote fixings the same—creamy dressing with Tajín seasoning and the delicious salty cotija cheese—which makes this salad absolute perfection.

For the Dressing

¼ cup sour cream

¼ cup mayonnaise

1 teaspoon granulated sugar

1 lime, zested and juiced

1 clove garlic, minced

1 teaspoon Tajín seasoning (found in the Mexican food aisle)

For the Salad

3 to 4 cups cooked or grilled corn

1 pint cherry tomatoes, halved

1 bunch cilantro, chopped, plus more for garnish

½ cup diced red onion

1 jalapeño, seeded and diced

½ cup cotija cheese

1. To make the dressing: Whisk together the sour cream, mayonnaise, sugar, lime zest, lime juice, garlic, and Tajín seasoning. Reserve.

2. To make the salad: In a large bowl, stir together the corn, tomatoes, cilantro, red onion, jalapeño, and cotija cheese. Add a little dressing to the salad and toss to combine. Transfer the salad to a serving bowl, garnish with additional cilantro leaves, and serve with the dressing on the side.

CÓRIA ESTATES

LUIS, JANICE, AND AURORA CÓRIA / SALEM, OREGON

On a hilltop in the central Willamette Valley, with 360-degree views of the Oregon coast and Cascade Mountains, sits the prettiest little vineyard and tasting room, Cória Estates. Cória Estates is a family-owned boutique winery specializing in Pinot Noir, Pinot Gris, and Chardonnay.

Luis Cória and his wife, Janice, both come from families with rich farmiing histories. They continued the tradition and purchased their first nine acres of land in 1988. Not long after, in the early 1990s, they purchased a neighboring parcel with 70 acres of land. Because the land had nutrient-rich soil and was located in the perfect climate for growing cool-grape varietals, Luis and Janice decided to plant their first vineyard.

Over the next two decades, Luis expanded the vineyards and grew fruit for other wineries. But when Luis's youngest daughter, Aurora, became interested in winemaking, the Cória vineyards became more than just a farm. Aurora went back to school to learn the art of winemaking and is now the Cória Estates winemaker. In 2013, they bottled their first vintage with huge success.

Aurora Cória approaches winemaking with nature in mind. She wants to keep their wine as pure as possible and let the fruit speak for itself. Her goal is to allow the vintage to reflect the natural elements of each growing season.

Cória Estates is truly a jewel among wineries. Aurora says, "We want customers to experience our wine while surrounded by the warm and inviting ambiance of the winery." The tasting room reflects the vibrant Mexican heritage of the Cória family, along with majestic views of the Willamette Valley, a cozy fireplace for cool weather tastings, festive events with live music, wine and yoga pairings, food trucks during the warmer months, and, of course, lush and elegant Cória wine.

Oregon Shrimp Salad with Spicy Seafood Dressing

SERVES 4

There are times when all I crave on a hot summer evening is this simple Oregon Shrimp Salad with Spicy Seafood Dressing. It's crisp, cool, and completely fuss-free. I've kept it simple, using only ingredients that I absolutely adore: salad greens, cucumbers, olives, small shrimp, and Cheddar. That's it! I lightly dress it in a spicy seafood dressing that complements all the ingredients. I like to serve this salad with freshly baked rustic sourdough bread slices, olive oil, fresh lemon wedges, and a crisp white wine, such as Cória Estates Chardonnay.

For the Dressing

¾ cup mayonnaise

¼ cup chili sauce

Juice of 1 lemon

½ teaspoon prepared horseradish

1 teaspoon Worcestershire sauce

2 tablespoons finely chopped fresh chives

1 tablespoon chopped capers

Salt and pepper, to taste

For the Salad

2 romaine hearts, chopped

⅓ cup very thinly sliced cucumber

¼ cup sliced olives (or more to taste)

½ to ¾ pound small Oregon shrimp (often referred to as bay shrimp)

½ cup shredded Cheddar

Sliced green onions, for garnish

Lemon wedges, to serve

1. To make the dressing, mix together the mayonnaise, chili sauce, lemon juice, horseradish, Worcestershire, chives, and capers. Season to taste with salt and pepper.

2. To make the salad, divide the romaine between 4 plates. Top with the cucumber, olives, shrimp, and Cheddar. Garnish with sliced green onions and serve with lemon wedges and the dressing on the side.

Note: For a dressed salad, add the romaine to a large bowl and lightly dress the salad greens. Then divide among salad plates and top with remaining ingredients. Serve any extra dressing on the side.

Carrot and Cilantro Salad with Ginger and Sun Butter Dressing

SERVES 4 TO 6

Peanut butter has always been on my list of pantry staples. I especially love peanut butter in dressings and sauces for stir-fries or vegetables. At one point, however, my daughters developed a slight allergy to peanut butter, so I switched to sunflower seed butter. I actually prefer the taste over peanut butter.

You can find sunflower seed butter in the natural section of most markets. If you prefer peanut butter, however, that works just as well.

For the Dressing

¼ cup sunflower seed butter (or peanut butter)

2 teaspoons grated fresh ginger

1 clove garlic

¼ cup honey

2 teaspoons soy sauce, tamari, or coconut aminos

1 tablespoon rice vinegar

Squeeze of fresh lime juice (about 1 tablespoon)

¼ cup water, or more for desired consistency

Dash of chili sauce, sriracha, or Thai chili sauce
    (optional)

For the Salad

4 cups shredded carrots

¾ cup (1 bunch) cilantro, plus more for garnish

¼ cup pumpkin seeds, raw or toasted, plus more
    for garnish

2 tablespoons sesame seeds, plus more for garnish

1. Place all the dressing ingredients into a blender or food processor and blend until the dressing is smooth. (For a little heat, include the chili sauce.) If it feels too thick, add additional water, one or two tablespoons at a time.

2. In a large bowl, toss together the shredded carrots, cilantro, and seeds. (Do not add the dressing until you are ready to serve.) Add just enough dressing to the carrot mixture to coat the carrots. Don't over-dress the salad but, rather, serve the remaining dressing with the salad.

3. Pour the salad into a serving bowl or onto a serving platter and garnish with extra cilantro and seeds.

Note: The Ginger and Sun Butter Dressing makes a great marinade for shrimp, chicken, or a veggie salad bowl.

Braised Red Cabbage with Apples and Bacon

SERVES 4 TO 6

Apples grow with wild abandon in Oregon. It seems almost every farm has an apple tree or two; they can often be found in suburban backyards, along city streets, and in parks. Although Oregon grows a delicious variety of heirloom apples such as Ashmead's Kernel or the Arkansas Black, Fuji, Gala, and Honeycrisp are the most popular varieties grown here.

Because apples are a large crop in Oregon, they find their way into all sorts of drinks and food, from cider to this Braised Red Cabbage. I think apples, bacon, and cabbage make a flavorful combination of ingredients, which pair well with grilled sausages or pork chops. This is also a lovely recipe when served with a slow-roasted pork roast or roast chicken.

2 tablespoons ghee

4 ounces bacon, diced

1 red onion, halved and thinly sliced

1 medium head red cabbage, cored and shredded

2 cloves garlic, minced

¼ cup apple cider vinegar or balsamic vinegar

¼ to ½ cup vegetable broth

1 tablespoon granulated sugar

1 apple, cored and diced

Salt and pepper, to taste

Chopped fresh parsley, for garnish

1. Preheat the oven to 350°F.

2. In an ovenproof skillet or Dutch oven, heat 1 tablespoon of ghee over medium-high heat. Add the diced bacon and cook until the bacon is crispy and the fat is rendered.

3. Remove the bacon from the pan and set aside. Remove all but 2 tablespoons of fat from the pan.

4. Add the onion, cabbage, and garlic to the pan. Cook for 5 to 8 minutes until the cabbage begins to wilt. Add the bacon back into the pan.

5. Stir in the vinegar, vegetable broth, sugar, and apple. Bring the liquid to a boil and then cover the skillet or Dutch oven with a lid and place it in the oven for about 45 minutes. Give the cabbage a little stir about every 15 minutes or so.

6. Remove the cabbage from the oven, stir in the last tablespoon of ghee, and season to taste with salt and pepper. Garnish with the parsley and serve.

Orange Marmalade and Miso Roasted Carrots with Toasted Sesame Seeds

SERVES 4 TO 6

There is nothing more delicious than farm-fresh produce, which is what The Croft Farm on Sauvie Island does best. It has a gorgeous farm garden, fresh honey, blueberries, and succulents. I left the farm craving this lovely roasted carrot recipe.

I love to make this recipe as an alternative to buttered or steamed carrots. I've tossed the carrots in a mixture of orange marmalade and miso paste with fresh ginger and garlic. Then I roast them to crisp tender and serve them with roast pork or chicken.

3 tablespoons white miso paste

¼ cup orange marmalade

2 tablespoons extra virgin olive oil

1 clove garlic, minced

1 teaspoon grated fresh ginger

1½ to 2 pounds carrots with carrot tops attached

Salt and pepper, to taste

Toasted sesame seeds for garnish (optional)

1 tablespoon minced parsley, for garnish (optional)

1. Preheat the oven to 400°F.

2. Line a baking sheet (or two if needed) with parchment paper. Whisk together the miso paste, marmalade, olive oil, garlic, and ginger.

3. Cut off the carrot tops, leaving about 2 inches of stems. Place the carrots in a large bowl and toss with the marmalade-miso mixture. Place the carrots on the parchment paper–lined baking sheet in a single layer and sprinkle with a little salt and pepper.

4. Cover the carrots with foil and roast for 25 to 30 minutes, then uncover the carrots and let them roast for another 15 to 20 minutes or until they are tender. I like my carrots crisp tender, so I take them out of the oven early.

5. As soon as they come out of the oven, sprinkle with the toasted sesame seeds, if using. Transfer the carrots to a platter and serve.

THE CROFT FARM

VAIL AND GREG / SAUVIE ISLAND, OREGON

I had the most delightful afternoon visit to The Croft Farm, which included warm hospitality and a cup of delicious tea while sitting outdoors under a blue summer sky. After spending some time talking with Vail, cofounder of The Croft Farm, it's clear she and her partner, Greg, have a deep love for the land, locally grown food, and their community.

Vail and Greg began The Croft Farm in 2013, after deciding they wanted to spend as much time as possible close to the soil, fresh food, non-human animals, and their children.

This quaint river-island farm is situated on a little over seven acres on Sauvie Island in Portland. Sauvie Island is a unique place where the Willamette and the Columbia Rivers converge—not quite remote, but not in the city either. Although it's almost twice the size of Manhattan, Sauvie Island only has about 1,000 residents and much of the island is a wildlife refuge.

The Croft Farm grows organic vegetables, U-pick summer blueberries, succulents, and crisp cider apples. They even make honey! They're also raising a sweet-natured rescue cow that is completely blind, her goat companions and guides, rescue alpacas, chickens, and sheep, whose wool they use for fiber to make yarn. In the summer, Greg and Vail operate a small artisan produce stand where they sell directly to families and small restaurants via their CSA (community supported agriculture) program.

In addition to the farm, Vail and Greg love sharing their knowledge and experience with others. They built a guest house on the farm where visitors can come stay and learn about diversified farming and low-impact, small-home living.

Vail says, "Our croft is a passionate labor of love for our small family. We *really* love what we do and how we live."

Lemon-Herb Roasted New Potatoes

SERVES 4

This was one of the first herb-infused recipes I learned to make while in culinary school. I remember being so proud of myself when I made this for the first time at home. It's truly a delicious potato recipe and one that I've been making for the last 20 years. I adore the lemon, basil, and parsley combination, but it's equally good with rosemary, thyme, and sage.

2 tablespoons extra virgin olive oil,
    plus more for serving

2 cloves garlic, minced

1½ pounds small red potatoes or fingerling potatoes

½ teaspoon salt

½ teaspoon black pepper

Zest of 1 lemon

¼ cup basil leaves, chiffonade

1 tablespoon chopped fresh parsley

1. Preheat the oven to 400°F.

2. In a large bowl, mix together the olive oil and garlic. Add the potatoes and toss to coat.

3. Pour the potatoes in a single layer onto a parchment paper–lined baking sheet and sprinkle with salt and pepper. Roast the potatoes for about 30 minutes, or until they are brown and crisp on the outside and soft on the inside.

4. Remove the potatoes from the oven and let them cool for about 5 minutes. Then slightly smash them and place them in a bowl. Toss with the lemon zest, basil, and parsley. Drizzle with additional olive oil and season to taste with additional salt and pepper, if desired. Transfer the potatoes to a serving dish and serve warm.

Note: To chiffonade herbs, stack the leaves, roll into a cigar shape, and then slice into ribbons.

Winter Vegetable Gratin

SERVES 8 TO 10

I adore a gratin any season of the year, but especially during the cooler months. This winter vegetable gratin is filled with four layers of my favorites: sweet potatoes, yellow potatoes, turnips, and rutabaga. It's baked in an herb-and-garlic–laced heavy cream and topped with more decadence—cheese! It's a gorgeous winter vegetable dish to serve dinner guests, or for Sunday dinner with the family.

2 cups heavy cream

½ cup chicken broth

1 tablespoon assorted chopped herbs: rosemary, sage, thyme, and parsley

4 cloves garlic, minced

1½ to 2 pounds sweet potatoes

½ pound rutabaga

½ pound turnips

1 pound yellow potatoes

1 tablespoon unsalted butter

2 cups shredded Swiss or Gruyère cheese

Salt and pepper, to taste

1. Preheat the oven to 400°F.

2. Add the heavy cream, chicken broth, herbs, and garlic to a pan over low heat. Bring the cream to a low simmer and then take it off the heat.

3. Thinly slice all the vegetables. I use a mandoline slicer set on 4.5 millimeters. Slicing the vegetables evenly ensures they all cook evenly. Butter the bottom of a 9-by-11-inch or 9-by-13-inch baking dish. I prefer a deep baking dish so that I can achieve four to five layers.

4. Place a layer of sweet potatoes on the bottom and then ladle a little of the herb-and-garlic cream over the potatoes. Season with a pinch of salt and pepper and sprinkle with a little of the shredded cheese.

Repeat the same steps with a layer of rutabaga, then the turnips, next the potatoes, and top with a last layer of sweet potatoes or whatever you might have left. Top with the remaining shredded cheese.

5. Wrap foil over the baking dish and place the baking dish on a baking sheet, just in case the cream bubbles over. Bake the gratin for 1 hour. Then take the foil off the gratin and bake for another 15 minutes to caramelize the top.

6. Remove from the oven and let it cool for about 15 minutes before serving.

Whole Roasted Cauliflower with Creamy Cheese Sauce

SERVES 4 TO 6

The farmers of Moon River Farm (or the cruciferous sisters, as I like to call them) grow many delightful vegetables that are quite popular in recipes these days. One cruciferous vegetable that is getting a lot of attention lately is cauliflower.

Although cauliflower has made a victorious comeback, I've been a fan of this delicious vegetable for a long time. Years ago, my lovely friend Margaret made a whole roasted cauliflower for a dinner party at her home. It was so delicious, even my two young daughters loved it.

I started making it at my home and eventually added a cheese sauce to the recipe. My family loves a sauce over their vegetables, so a creamy, comforting cheese sauce seemed like a perfect addition to this roasted cauliflower. I slice the baked cauliflower in thick slices, layer the slices on a platter, and drizzle with the creamy, garlic-spiked cheese sauce. If you have extra sauce, serve it on the side. Although this recipe is lovely with the cheese sauce, it's just as delicious served with a drizzle of extra virgin olive oil or a pat of butter.

For the Cauliflower

1 head cauliflower, rinsed and dried

2 tablespoons extra virgin olive oil

½ teaspoon salt

½ teaspoon pepper

For the Cheese Sauce

4 tablespoons (½ stick) unsalted butter

1 clove garlic, minced

2 tablespoons all-purpose flour

1½ cups whole milk, warm or room temperature

½ cup chicken or vegetable broth

¼ teaspoon dry mustard

¼ teaspoon ground nutmeg

1 cup shredded Cheddar

Salt and pepper, to taste

1 tablespoon chopped fresh parsley, for garnish

1. Preheat the oven to 425°F.

2. Trim the leaves from the bottom of the cauliflower and trim off the center core so the cauliflower will sit on the bottom of a baking dish.

3. Place the cauliflower in a baking dish and rub it with the extra virgin olive oil and season with salt and pepper.

4. Tent foil over the baking dish and cauliflower, pinching the foil gently around the edges of the baking dish. It doesn't have to be a tight cover. Bake for 40 minutes. After 40 minutes, remove the foil and let the cauliflower bake uncovered for an additional 20 minutes. The cauliflower is done when a knife is easily pressed into the center.

5. To make the sauce, heat a skillet over medium heat. Add the butter. When the butter is melted, add the garlic and then whisk in the flour. Cook for about 1 minute. Then slowly whisk in the milk and broth. Bring the sauce to a boil and simmer on low until thickened. Take the skillet off the heat and stir in the dry mustard, ground nutmeg, and Cheddar. Season to taste with salt and pepper.

6. To serve, place the whole cauliflower on a serving dish and slice into serving-size slices, then drizzle the cheese sauce over the top. Garnish with fresh chopped parsley. Serve warm.

MOON RIVER FARM

KAYLEIGH HILLERT AND LILY STRAUSS / NEHALEM, OREGON

Moon River Farm is a small, women-owned vegetable farm on the beautiful north Oregon coast. It's surrounded by forest, rivers, valleys, and the majestic Pacific Ocean. The cool weather climate allows farmers Lily and Kayleigh to grow 50 varieties of vegetables from May through October.

You could say both Lily and Kayleigh have farming in their blood. Lily is the descendent of Swiss immigrant dairy farmers in Missouri and Mennonite farmers in California, and Kayleigh grew up with summer visits to her grandparents' 100-year-old dairy farm. They both earned college degrees and, from that point on, they found themselves immersed in the adventures of farming.

They both joined WWOOF (Willing Workers On Organic Farms) and eventually met at a local farm called R-Evolution Gardens. It was during that time that Lily and Kayleigh realized farming would be their future. They fell in love with the north coast of Oregon and, together, they decided to follow their passion for small-scale vegetable farming and formed Moon River Farm.

Lily and Kayleigh believe in growing food in a way that supports all the living systems that surround and support their farm. They employ practices that allow them to grow food without the use of pesticides, herbicides, or fungicides. They also utilize low-till/no-till practices and reduce their reliance on fossil fuels by farming primarily by hand.

Kayleigh and Lily say, "We feel strongly about providing our wonderful coastal community with local, safe, healthy, fresh food."

You can find Moon River Farm produce through their CSA (community supported agriculture), the Manzanita Farmers' Market, and local restaurants.

Creamed Swiss Chard

SERVES 4

Leafy greens thrive in the Oregon soil and mild Oregon temperatures. It's the only place I've lived where I can start greens in my garden in early spring and they keep growing until the first freeze of winter. Because greens grow so well here, our farmers' markets and co-op markets are always filled with the most beautiful, fresh leafy greens.

Although spinach is typically used in this recipe, I've also used mustard greens, collards, kale, and dandelion greens. However, I really like this recipe with Swiss chard. Swiss chard is hearty and doesn't wilt quite as much as spinach, and it's got a bolder flavor that can also have some bitterness. The bitterness usually mellows with cooking and, when combined with leeks, garlic, and cream, the Swiss chard becomes slightly sweet and robust.

This dish is really sort of a gratin, but I prepare and serve it in a skillet. It feels very "homestyle" and comforting, especially when served alongside a Sunday beef roast or roast chicken.

¼ cup panko bread crumbs

¼ cup grated Parmesan

1 tablespoon unsalted butter

1 tablespoon extra virgin olive oil

2 medium leeks, trimmed just where the light green turns to dark green, cut in half lengthwise, rinsed, and diced

1 teaspoon chopped fresh Italian parsley

1 to 2 cloves garlic, minced

2 bunches (about 2 pounds) Swiss chard, stems removed (I save the stems for stock or soup), leaves coarsely chopped

½ teaspoon grated nutmeg

½ to 1 teaspoon salt

½ teaspoon black pepper

1 cup heavy whipping cream

1. Preheat the oven to 375°F. Mix together the panko bread crumbs and grated Parmesan. Set aside.

2. In a large oven-safe sauté pan or skillet, add the butter and olive oil to the pan and place the pan over medium-high heat.

3. Once the butter is melted and oil is hot, add the leeks and Italian parsley, sautéing until wilted and slightly golden. Stir in the minced garlic and sauté for 1 minute longer.

4. With tongs, add the chopped Swiss chard in batches to the pan and toss with the leeks, continuing to toss the greens and leeks gently, until all the greens are in the pan and wilted. Sprinkle with grated nutmeg and season with salt and black pepper.

5. Pour the heavy cream into the pan and gently toss with the greens. Sprinkle the panko-Parmesan mixture over the top of the creamed Swiss chard and then place the pan in the oven.

6. Let the creamed Swiss chard bake for 15 to 20 minutes or until the sides are bubbly and the cream has thickened. To toast the panko-Parmesan mixture, set the pan under the broiler for just a few minutes.

7. Remove from the oven and let the creamed Swiss chard sit for about 5 minutes before serving.

MARION POLK FOOD SHARE YOUTH FARM

JARED HIBBARD-SWANSON / SALEM, OREGON

Urban and community gardens have become more common over the last decade, and now Oregon can add a youth farm to this growing list of food producers. Marion Polk Food Share Youth Farm is a collaborative educational site that is working to cultivate a new generation of leaders by engaging young people in farming for the community.

The youth farmers grow more than 50 types of fruits and vegetables and the farm features production fields, an orchard, a learning garden, and a farm kitchen. The food is grown organically and then harvested and distributed to food pantries and health clinics that treat diet-related health issues and food insecurity, as well as the youth farmers and their families.

Youth Farm Manager Jared Hibbard-Swanson told me that when they began this small 6-acre urban farm, he was often asked if they were training the next generation of farmers. It would seem to be a natural fit, but what they also found was that, while the youth farmers were growing and harvesting food, they were also learn-

ing how to cook that food, gaining leadership skills, boosting confidence, and realizing they can each have a positive effect on the world.

According to Farm Coordinator Emily Griffith, the farm grows as much as 20,000 pounds of food every year. It was obvious when I spoke with a few of the youth farmers that they are excited about working the farm and growing their own food. They are proud that they're learning to cook and eat food they never thought they'd like but have now grown to love. They also feel proud that their work on the farm allows them to support their community in one of the most important ways—by providing food to those in need.

Roasted Green Bean Salad with Dried Cherries, Toasted Pine Nuts, and Goat Cheese

SERVES 4

As I was talking to the student farmers at the Marion Polk Food Share Youth Farm, they mentioned how much they love cooking the food they grow. Many of the students commented that they never knew how much they liked vegetables until they started cooking them to use in their farm lunches.

Roasting vegetables such as green beans creates a slightly sweet flavor, and the browned bits add a hint of caramel notes. While this makes them perfect for more familiar recipes like pizza or flatbread, the young farmers from Marion Polk Youth Farm have learned to appreciate snacking on them right off the baking sheet. Roasted green beans also make a delicious base for this impressive warm salad that I've finished with dried cherries, pine nuts, and goat cheese.

For the Salad

1 pound fresh green beans, washed, trimmed, and patted dry

1 tablespoon extra virgin olive oil

Pinch each of salt and black pepper

4 ounces smoked goat cheese, or more to taste (if you can't find smoked goat cheese, feel free to substitute with your favorite soft goat cheese)

½ cup dried cherries

¼ cup pine nuts, lightly toasted

For the Dressing

3 tablespoons high-quality balsamic vinegar

½ cup extra virgin olive oil

1 tablespoon honey

1 teaspoon Dijon mustard

Salt and cracked black pepper, to taste

1. Preheat the oven to 400°F.

2. Toss the green beans in the olive oil and spread them in a single layer on a baking sheet. Sprinkle with a pinch of salt and pepper. Place the baking sheet in the oven and roast the beans for 15 to 20 minutes, or until they begin to shrivel and are slightly toasted.

3. To make the dressing: In a small bowl, add the vinegar, olive oil, honey, and Dijon mustard. Whisk together until nicely combined. Season to taste with salt and pepper.

4. To assemble the salad, arrange the warm green beans on a platter. Drizzle the dressing over the green beans and sprinkle with crumbled goat cheese, dried cherries, and toasted pine nuts.

Note: Serve as a side dish with meat, poultry, or seafood. This is also lovely as a main dish over a bed of mixed greens and a few more veggies, such as pickled beets and roasted carrots.

Chermoula-Marinated Grilled Vegetable and Pineapple Skewers

SERVES 4 TO 6

What could be more mouthwatering than a summer barbecue with a side of grilled vegetable skewers? The answer is a side of vegetable skewers drizzled with this gorgeous Chermoula-style sauce.

Grilled vegetable skewers are a summer staple, and although they make a beautiful presentation and complement a variety of entrées, I love them most when they are served with this sauce. This is a Moroccan sauce traditionally served with fish or vegetables. It reminds me of a Spanish salsa verde, a French pistou, or an Italian pesto, all made with fresh herbs, lemon, garlic, and other fragrant spices.

To mix flavors up a bit, I've added cubes of pineapple for a savory, sweet, and herb-laced finish. These skewers are as delicious as they are beautiful.

For the Chermoula Marinade

½ cup fresh cilantro

½ cup fresh Italian parsley

1 tablespoon capers

2 cloves garlic

1 teaspoon grated fresh ginger

1½ teaspoons smoked paprika

Zest and juice of 1 lemon

½ cup extra virgin olive oil

Salt and pepper, to taste

For the Skewers

1 red or orange bell pepper, cut into chunks

1 red onion, cut into chunks

1 small zucchini, sliced into rounds

1 small yellow squash, sliced into rounds

10 small cremini mushrooms

2 cups cubed fresh pineapple

1. Add the cilantro, parsley, capers, garlic, ginger, smoked paprika, lemon zest, lemon juice, and olive oil to the bowl of a food processor or blender. Puree until slightly smooth. Season to taste with salt and pepper.

2. Using skewers for a grill, skewer the vegetables and pineapple, leaving a small space between each piece, and then lay them on a parchment paper–lined baking sheet. Brush the skewers with some of the sauce and let them sit for about 15 minutes while you preheat the grill.

3. Preheat the grill to 400°F. When the grill is hot, oil down the grates to prevent sticking. Cook on the grill for 5 to 8 minutes each side, or 10 to 16 minutes total, until the vegetables are crisp tender.

4. Transfer the skewers to a platter and drizzle some of the sauce over the skewers. Serve warm with any remaining sauce.

Baked Summer Squash Tian

SERVES 4 TO 6

Traditionally, a tian is a meal prepared in a Provençal earthenware dish, which is also referred to as a *tian*. Today you'll find many recipes that bear this name. The dishes often have uniform-shaped ingredients arranged in rows or circles and are typically topped with cheese or heavy cream and sometimes even tomato sauce. A tian is such a lovely and delicious way to use all of our Oregon summer squash.

For this tian, I've arranged summer squash in a baking dish with leeks, garlic, and olive oil and then topped it with bread crumbs and grated Parmesan. It's a simple and delicious recipe, easily adapted to use your favorite summer squash.

1 tablespoon unsalted butter

1 to 1½ pounds summer squash or zucchini (yellow or green), sliced into rounds about ¼ inch thick

2 tablespoons extra virgin olive oil

1 leek, white part only, washed and chopped

3 cloves garlic, minced

1 teaspoon fresh chopped thyme

1 tablespoon fresh chopped parsley

½ teaspoon salt

½ teaspoon pepper

2 tablespoons grated Parmesan

1 tablespoon Italian bread crumbs

1. Preheat the oven to 375°F.

2. Butter an 8-by-10-inch oval or 9-inch round or 8-inch square baking dish. Place the sliced squash in a large bowl.

3. In a medium skillet over medium heat, add the olive oil and, when the oil is hot, add the chopped leeks. Cook the leeks over medium heat until they are soft and slightly golden, about 5 minutes. Stir in garlic, thyme, and parsley and cook 1 minute longer. Take the skillet off the heat and pour the leeks and garlic over the squash and season with salt and pepper.

4. Layer the circles of squash sort of standing up leaning against each other in rows, or in a circle if using a round pan. Once you've packed all the squash in the baking dish, sprinkle any remaining cooked leeks over the squash.

5. Mix together the Parmesan and bread crumbs and sprinkle over the vegetables. Bake in the oven for 10 to 15 minutes or until the bread and cheese are golden on top. The squash should be crisp tender.

6. Remove the baking dish from the oven and let the squash cool slightly before serving.

ENTRÉES

Fennel and Sausage Carbonara

SERVES 4

If you've ever been wary of making a carbonara, now is the time to try one. I adore carbonara, but it can be a fussy dish to prepare.

Thankfully, I believe I've created an approachable recipe for every level of home cook. As an added security measure, I ran the recipe by one of my favorite chefs, Nathan Rafn of Rafns' Restaurant in Salem, Oregon. During my interview with Chef Nathan, I mentioned I was having a little trouble making this recipe more achievable for home cooks. So he invited me into his restaurant kitchen for a little recipe testing and a class on methods for making carbonara.

I was anxious to practice what I learned, so when I arrived home, I employed a few of his recommendations and this version of carbonara was born. I'm proud to say it's one of the most luscious pasta recipes I've tasted.

12 ounces penne, cavatelli, strozzapreti, or orecchiette

2 tablespoons salt, plus more to taste

1 tablespoon extra virgin olive oil

1 pound ground Italian sausage, hot or sweet

1 large fennel bulb, thinly shaved; reserve a tablespoon of fennel fronds for garnish

4 to 6 cloves garlic, minced

1 tablespoon fresh chopped Italian parsley, plus more for garnish

Pinch of crushed red pepper flakes (optional)

¼ cup warmed heavy cream

½ cup pasta water, divided

2 eggs, room temperature

¼ cup grated Parmigiano-Reggiano, plus more for garnish

Freshly cracked black pepper, to taste

Juice of 1 lemon

Lemon wedges, to serve

continued . . .

1. Cook the pasta al dente according to package directions. Add 2 tablespoons of salt to the pasta water. Reserve ½ cup of the pasta water when the pasta is done.

2. While the pasta water is coming to a boil, heat the olive oil in a large skillet over medium heat. Add the ground sausage and cook through, but don't overcook. With a mesh spoon, transfer the sausage to a plate.

3. Leave about 1 tablespoon of oil in the skillet and add the shaved fennel. Sauté over medium heat until the fennel is soft and slightly caramelized, about 10 to 12 minutes. Stir in the garlic, Italian parsley, and red pepper flakes (if using), and sauté for 1 minute longer.

4. Add the sausage back to the skillet and stir to combine. Take the pan off the heat and fold the cooked pasta into the sausage-fennel mixture.

5. In a bowl or large measuring cup, whisk together the warm heavy cream and only ¼ cup pasta water to start; you can add more water if needed later. In another bowl, whisk the two room-temperature eggs. While you continue to whisk the eggs, slowly drizzle the warm cream and pasta water into the eggs. This will temper the eggs and keep them from cooking when added to the pasta. Whisk in the grated Parmesan.

6. Pour the sauce over the pasta and toss to combine. Season to taste with salt and black pepper, give it a squeeze of lemon, and garnish with additional chopped parsley, fennel fronds, and grated cheese. Serve immediately with lemon wedges.

Side Dish Recommendations: Roasted Winter Beet Salad with Candied Nuts and Blue Cheese (page 93), Oregon Shrimp Salad with Spicy Seafood Dressing (page 101), Blackberry Burrata Salad (page 96)

Lemon Risotto with Crispy Mushrooms and Fresh Herbs

SERVES 4

I've spent the better part of 20 years making risotto. It was one of the first recipes I learned to make after culinary school, and it's continued to be a favorite dinner for my family. Thus, I probably make 20 different versions of risotto that include various seasonal ingredients or ingredients my family enjoys.

Lemon Risotto with Crispy Mushrooms and Fresh Herbs is what I call my "everyday" risotto. It's the risotto I make when my daughters need a giant food hug or when I'm in need of simplicity with a smidgen of indulgence.

Complemented by a subtle hint of citrus and topped with mushrooms lightly fried in butter and olive oil while bathing in fresh herbs, this just might become your "everyday" risotto too. I adore this risotto paired with a crisp Chardonnay from Willamette Valley Vineyards.

For the Broth

4 cups chicken or vegetable broth

One 3-inch sprig fresh thyme

1 bay leaf

One 2-inch piece Parmesan rind (optional but it makes the broth taste delicious)

For the Mushrooms

1 tablespoon extra virgin olive oil

1 tablespoon unsalted butter

2 cups sliced fresh seasonal mushrooms

1 clove garlic, minced

1 tablespoon chopped fresh mint

1 tablespoon chopped fresh basil

1 tablespoon chopped fresh parsley

Juice of 1 lemon

Salt and pepper, to taste

For the Risotto

2 tablespoons extra virgin olive oil or butter

½ yellow onion, finely diced

1 clove garlic, minced

1 cup Arborio or Carnaroli rice

½ cup dry white wine

¾ cup grated Parmesan

2 tablespoons unsalted butter

Zest of 1 lemon

Salt and pepper, to taste

1. In a soup pot over low heat, add the broth, fresh thyme, bay leaf, and Parmesan rind. Let the broth simmer.

2. Prepare the mushrooms. Heat a large skillet over medium heat and add the olive oil and butter. When the oil-butter is hot, add the mushrooms and sauté until slightly browned and a little crispy. Then stir in the garlic, herbs, and lemon juice and immediately take the skillet off the heat so the garlic doesn't brown. Season lightly with a bit of salt and pepper. Transfer to a bowl and reserve.

3. Prepare the risotto. In a Dutch oven or large pot over medium heat, add the olive oil or butter. Stir in the onion and cook until slightly softened. Stir in the garlic and rice and cook for 1 minute longer.

4. Add the wine and stir until the wine is almost absorbed. Stir in about 1 cup of the simmering chicken broth (don't add the herbs or Parmesan) and continue to stir constantly until the liquid is almost absorbed.

5. Continue to repeat this process with ½ cup of broth at a time, stirring constantly and allowing each addition of broth to be absorbed before adding the next ½ cup. This process should take 20 to 30 minutes or until the rice is almost tender.

6. When the risotto is done, take it off the heat and stir in the grated Parmesan, butter, and lemon zest. Season to taste with salt and pepper.

7. Divide the risotto into four bowls and top each bowl with the crispy mushrooms and herbs. Serve immediately.

Side Dish Recommendation: Blackberry Burrata Salad (page 96)

CHEF NATHAN RAFN

RAFNS' RESTAURANT / SALEM, OREGON

After dining at Rafns' several times, it became clear to me that Chef Nathan Rafn was born to cook. Rafns' is a small, charming restaurant in downtown Salem that politely boasts a decor of comfortable elegance and an elevated dining experience so delightful, one is not likely to forget.

Over the last six years, Chef Nate has been creating a menu of farm-fresh, mostly Italian-inspired dishes with creative twists. I can personally tell you the risotto is perfectly al dente with a silky and creamy texture and the Bolognese is rich, almost decadent, and slow-cooked to perfection. Along with a drool-worthy menu is an impressive cocktail and wine list that is not to be missed.

Chef Nathan Rafn began his cooking career as an apprentice at a well-known Italian restaurant in the Salem area. Although he started by busing tables and washing dishes, it wasn't long before he got the opportunity to work in the kitchen as a chef apprentice.

While he apprenticed at the restaurant, Chef Nate started an invitation-only supper club for which he sourced local ingredients and featured one farmer for each dinner. His love of local farms and the food they produce later inspired Chef Nate to create a local television show that ran from 2006 to 2013 where he interviewed farmers and chefs around the state.

Inspired by his work as a chef apprentice, working with local farmers for his supper club, and conducting farmer interviews, Chef Nate decided it was time to open his own restaurant. In 2013, together with his wife and business partner, Rochelle Rafn, Chef Nate opened Rafns' in downtown Salem.

I met Chef Nate at his restaurant and found him to be humble, thoughtful, and a person who exemplifies a culinary brilliance that results in some of the best dining in the Willamette Valley. His goal has always been to create an elevated dining experience with excellent service and continual support for our local farmers. Rafns' Restaurant is dedicated to using locally sourced, seasonal, and fresh ingredients along with artisinal foods created with love and care from the Pacific Northwest, France, and Italy.

Spiced Ground Turkey and Apple-Stuffed Winter Squash

SERVES 4

When winter squash season arrives in Oregon, I find myself dreaming up all sorts of new ways to use them. This is one of those recipes that was born out of buying too many winter squash at a fall farmers' market one year.

I originally created this recipe without the meat and served it as a side dish or a vegetarian entrée option. To make this heartier version, I added ground dark meat turkey, which pairs deliciously with the spices and apples. It's a fragrant and delectable recipe that also looks pretty on the plate.

2 to 3 winter squash, such as acorn, delicata, pumpkin, carnival, or butternut, halved lengthwise and seeds removed

1 tablespoon olive oil

2 tablespoons coconut oil

1 medium onion, diced

1 medium leek, white part only, diced

1 pound ground dark meat turkey (or ground chicken)

3 cloves garlic, minced

1 teaspoon salt

1 teaspoon grated fresh ginger

1 tablespoon curry powder

1 teaspoon garam masala

2 tablespoons brown sugar

¼ cup chopped fresh cilantro, plus two tablespoons for garnish

1 teaspoon apple cider vinegar

¾ cup diced apples

1 cup cooked rice, such as wild rice, jasmine, basmati, black, or red rice

Salt and pepper, to taste

1. Preheat the oven to 400°F.

2. With a good knife, cut just a bit off the bottom of each squash half so that it will sit nicely upright in order to hold the filling.

3. Brush each squash half with olive oil and then place them flesh side down on a baking sheet. Bake in the oven for about 45 minutes, or until the flesh is soft. While the squash is baking, prepare the filling.

4. In a large skillet over medium-high heat, add the coconut oil. When the oil is hot, add the onion and leek, and sauté until softened. Stir in the ground turkey. Cook the turkey until it's almost done, and then add the garlic, salt, ginger, curry powder, garam masala, brown sugar, cilantro, and apple cider vinegar.

5. Once the ingredients are incorporated, take the skillet off the heat and stir in the apples and cooked rice. Taste for seasoning.

6. When the squash are done, allow them to cool slightly. Then fill each half with the turkey-and-apple filling and garnish with cilantro.

Note: The squash can be baked a day in advance. Keep them in the refrigerator until needed. Warm the squash in the oven before filling them.

Side Dish Recommendations: If you'd like to serve something in addition, my Carrot and Cilantro Salad with Ginger and Sun Butter Dressing (page 102) pairs nicely and the Sweet Pea and Feta Fritters with Chive Oil and Sour Cream (page 45) can be a tasty starter to this dish.

WILLAMETTE VALLEY VINEYARDS

JIM BERNAU / TURNER, OREGON

Located in Turner, Oregon, just off I-5, Willamette Valley Vineyards is perched on a rolling mountainside overlooking miles of lush green valley below. The meandering road that leads to the estate tasting room is fringed by vineyards of Chardonnay and Pinot Noir grapes and a patch of old-growth forest. On occasion, barn owls and hawks can even be spotted flying overhead. Inside the tasting room, the decor is elegant, warm, and inviting, with majestic views of the Willamette Valley.

Willamette Valley Vineyards was founded in 1983 by Oregon native Jim Bernau. His vision was to create world-class Pinot Noir from the Willamette Valley Appellation. Because the Willamette Valley's soil is rich with nutrients and the climate is typically cool and wet, it provides the perfect conditions for growing cool-climate varietals such as Pinot Noir and Chardonay grapes.

In addition to creating elegant, classic Oregon wine, stewardship of the land has been a principal focus in Willamette Valley Vineyards' winemaking. For several decades, they have been leading the way in environmental sustainability with conservation efforts that preserve the natural resources of the region. The use of wind and solar power, biodiesel, supporting native bee populations, and using barn owls and kestrels for pest control are just a few of the winery's many environmentally sustainable practices.

If the exquisite wine, magical venue, and earth-loving practices aren't enough, Willamette Valley Vineyards is also actively involved in supporting community and regional organizations. In 2018, they formed Oregon Solidarity along with King Estate Winery to help southern Oregon winemakers save their crops. It's community outreach and support like this that exemplifies the generous Oregon spirit.

Mushroom Bolognese

SERVES 4

Willamette Valley is home to a handful of farmers who grow and cultivate mushrooms, and it's also one of the best places to forage for wild mushrooms.

Due to our abundance of these glorious fungi, I created this lovely Bolognese to satiate my craving for mushrooms, and it just so happens to pair deliciously with a Willamette Valley Vineyards Pinot Noir.

This recipe is much like a classic Bolognese, although the sauce doesn't require as much time on the stovetop. I serve it over spaghetti, but it's also delightful served with homemade pappardelle.

1 ounce dried porcini mushrooms

1 cup boiling water

2 to 4 tablespoons extra virgin olive oil

1 large yellow onion, diced

2 medium carrots, diced

2 ribs celery, diced

4 medium to large cloves garlic, minced

½ teaspoon dried thyme (or 1 teaspoon chopped fresh thyme)

½ teaspoon dried oregano (or 1 teaspoon chopped fresh oregano)

1 tablespoon chopped fresh parsley

1 pound assorted fresh mushrooms, such as shiitake, oyster, chanterelle, maitake, cremini (don't use white button mushrooms), finely chopped

1 cup red wine (Pinot Noir works well)

Two 15-ounce cans tomato sauce (not pasta sauce)

Pinch of crushed red pepper

Salt and pepper, to taste

1 teaspoon granulated sugar (optional)

¼ cup heavy cream

12 ounces cooked spaghetti, linguine, pappardelle, or fettuccine

½ cup grated or shaved Parmesan or Pecorino Romano

Chopped fresh parsley or basil, for garnish

1. Place the dried porcini mushrooms in a heat-proof bowl and pour the boiling water over the mushrooms. Cover them to keep the heat in and let them sit for about 15 minutes, or until soft. Carefully spoon the mushrooms out of the hot water and finely chop them. Reserve ½ cup of the mushroom water.

2. In a large skillet over medium heat, add the olive oil. When the oil is hot but not smoking, add the onion, carrots, and celery. Sauté the vegetables for 5 to 8 minutes, or until soft.

3. Stir in the garlic, thyme, oregano, parsley, and assorted chopped mushrooms. Add an additional 1 to 2 tablespoons olive oil, if needed. Sauté the vegetables and mushrooms until they are soft and slightly golden brown. A little color on the vegetables and mushrooms will create a depth of flavor. Stir in the porcini mushrooms and take the skillet off the heat to stir in the red wine. Place the skillet back on low heat and let the wine reduce by half.

4. With the heat on low, stir in the tomato sauce and crushed red pepper. Let the sauce come to a slow boil and then turn down the heat to a simmer for 5 to 8 minutes, or until the sauce is nicely heated through. Season to taste with salt and pepper. At this point, add the sugar (if using) to the mixture to reduce some of the acid. Stir in the heavy cream. If the sauce feels too thick, stir in some of the reserved liquid from the mushrooms.

5. Take the skillet off the heat and let the Bolognese sit for about 5 minutes to allow all the flavors to meld together. Serve over cooked pasta with a generous helping of grated Parmesan or Pecorino Romano and chopped fresh parsley or basil.

Side Dish Recommendations: Roasted Green Bean Salad with Dried Cherries, Toasted Pine Nuts, and Goat Cheese (page 114) or Blackberry Burrata Salad (page 96)

Winter Vegetable Cobbler with Chive Cream Biscuits

SERVES 6

I am a biscuit gal at heart, so any opportunity to serve biscuits with dinner, or in the dinner—count me in. I wanted to create a savory winter cobbler so tasty, the meat would never be missed. I think I achieved my goal. This cobbler is filled with seasonal, farm-fresh flavors, a slightly creamy sauce, fresh herbs, and topped with chive-and-cream-laced biscuits. Truly comfort food at its finest.

For the Cobbler

3 tablespoons ghee or avocado oil

1 medium leek, white part only, halved, rinsed, and chopped

1 onion, diced

4 cloves garlic, minced

½ pound assorted mushrooms (cremini, shiitake, and chanterelle work well in this recipe)

2 tablespoons all-purpose flour

3 to 4 cups vegetable or chicken broth

1 teaspoon chopped fresh thyme

1 teaspoon chopped fresh sage

1 teaspoon chopped fresh rosemary

1 tablespoon chopped fresh parsley

2 pounds (about 3 cups) butternut squash, peeled, seeded, and cut into small bite-sized cubes

Salt and pepper, to taste

Chive Cream Biscuits

2 cups all-purpose flour

2 tablespoons baking powder

½ teaspoon salt

2 tablespoons chopped fresh chives

½ cup grated Cheddar (optional)

1½ cups heavy cream

1. Preheat the oven to 400°F.

2. Prepare the cobbler. Place the ghee in an ovenproof, heavy-bottomed pot or Dutch oven over medium heat. Add the leek and onion and sauté until softened, 2 to 3 minutes. Add the garlic and sauté 1 minute longer. Stir in the mushrooms and allow them to cook down and soften.

3. Stir in the flour and let it cook for 30 seconds to 1 minute, then slowly stir in the 3 cups broth. Add 1 additional cup of broth to thin the liquid, if necessary. Stir in thyme, sage, rosemary, parsley, and butternut squash. Taste for seasoning and add salt and pepper, if needed. Bring it to a simmer. Simmer on low until the squash is almost tender, 5 to 8 minutes.

4. Prepare the chive biscuits. Mix together the flour, baking powder, and salt. Stir in the chives, shredded Cheddar (if using), and heavy cream until combined.

5. Take the pot off the heat and drop the biscuits on top of the stew. Place the pot in the oven uncovered and bake for 12 to 15 minutes, or until biscuits are golden brown on top.

6. Remove from the oven and let cool. Serve warm.

Side Dish Recommendation: This lovely cobbler is a complete meal; however, should you want something to serve in addition, this recipe pairs deliciously with my Carrot and Cilantro Salad with Ginger and Sun Butter Dressing (page 102).

SAKÉONE

FOREST GROVE, OREGON

Did you know Oregon is home to the first US-owned-and-operated saké brewery/kura? There are now more than a dozen small-craft saké breweries in the United States; SakéOne, however, is one of the oldest and largest. SakéOne is nestled on the east slope of the Cascade Range in the north Willamette Valley, just outside Portland. Because the average rainfall there is 80 to 120 inches per year, SakéOne's founder knew that this abundance of water with excellent minerality would be the key to making excellent saké, which is traditionally brewed with the purest water possible.

SakéOne has been making their award-winning saké in Oregon for more than two decades. They craft three distinct product lines—Momokawa, Moonstone, and G—at the Forest Grove kura, and import a lovely selection of saké from friends and partners in Japan.

In addition to the kura, there is a lovely tasting room where visitors can sample each of the three product lines along with a wide range of traditional sakés. My first tasting at SakéOne was Moonstone, which is a junmai ginjo (which means "pure rice") saké with aromatic and bright natural flavors such as Asian pear and lemongrass. Momokawa is based on the age-old methods of Japanese teachers and is handcrafted with Oregon rain, which I think adds to the destinctive quality of this saké. The third is called G. This is where East meets West; while adhering to the traditions of fine Japanese saké, the G blend is also crafted to have big-layered flavors that the American palate has come to expect.

Whether you sip saké straight from the glass, mix it up in a cocktail, or use a splash for cooking, the makers of SakéOne strive to create the best-quality saké for the ultimate saké experience.

Miso Saké Glazed
Black Cod (Sablefish)

SERVES 4

It's funny how some fish are not really what we call them. While speaking to CSF Program Manager Mike Baran at Port Orford Sustainable Seafood, I kept talking about how much I love black cod. He informed me that black cod is actually sablefish or butterfish, which makes sense since it's a rich and buttery-tasting fish. Mike also mentioned this particular fish is called many different names across the world, but here in Oregon, most people refer to it as black cod.

If you find fresh black cod in your market, snag it! This recipe was inspired by my tastings at SakéOne, after a bottle of the Moonstone Coconut Lemongrass saké made its way home with me. After sipping it, I knew it would make the loveliest addition to this recipe. This particular saké adds a hint of coconut and lemongrass to the miso saké sauce and creates a slightly tropical flavor to the dish—but any saké you have on hand will do.

⅓ cup white miso paste

1½ tablespoons dark brown sugar

¼ to ⅓ cup high-quality saké

2 teaspoons minced fresh ginger

1 clove garlic, minced

½ teaspoon Thai Kitchen chili paste

1½ pounds black cod, cut into 4 pieces (or true cod, halibut, or any other firm white fish)

1 teaspoon unsalted butter or oil, for greasing

Freshly ground black pepper, to taste

Sliced green onion, for garnish (optional)

Jasmine or basmati rice, to serve

1. Heat the oven to 350°F.

2. In a food processor or blender, add the miso, brown sugar, saké, ginger, garlic, and Thai chili paste. Process until it's a smooth, slightly thick sauce. Add more saké to thin the sauce, if you'd like.

3. Place the fish in a buttered or oiled baking dish and season lightly with cracked black pepper. Spread the miso-saké glaze over the top of each piece of fish, and bake in the oven for 10 to 12 minutes. The rule of thumb with baking fish is: for every inch of thickness, bake it for 10 minutes. So, if it's a thicker piece of fish, you'll bake it for longer and if it's a thinner piece of fish you'll bake it for a shorter amount of time.

4. When the fish is done, transfer to plates or a platter and garnish with sliced green onions, if using, and serve with jasmine or basmati rice.

Side Dish Recommendation: Carrot and Cilantro Salad with Ginger and Sun Butter Dressing (page 102)

PORT ORFORD SUSTAINABLE SEAFOOD

PORT ORFORD, OREGON

From stunning seascapes to mountains with lush forests that meet the Pacific Ocean, Port Orford is the westernmost city in the contiguous United States. This small fishing community with impressive panoramic vistas sits on the coast of southern Oregon. It's also home to Port Orford Sustainable Seafood, one of only a handful of Community Supported Fisheries (CSF) in the United States..

Much like a farm CSA (community supported agriculture), Port Orford Sustainable Seafood sells locally caught seafood directly to consumers. Although one might think this is a normal practice for locally caught seafood, most of the seafood caught near Port Orford is processed 50 miles away and then shipped abroad by corporate buyers.

In an effort to retain some of the catch for the local community and provide high-quality, traceable fish to Oregonians, in 2009, fisherman and cofounder Aaron Longton and several colleagues formed Port Orford Sustainable Seafood.

I had the pleasure of speaking with Aaron, as well as CSF Program Manager Mike Baran, about the types of fresh seafood Port Orford Sustainable Seafood catches, processes, and delivers to consumers. For all the locals, note that they now have 12 different pick-up locations around the state.

Depending on the season, they offer Oregon Dungeness crab, Pacific octopus, ling cod, black cod, halibut, cabezon, rockfish (which has more than 74 species), Chinook salmon, and albacore tuna. Port Orford Sustainable Seafood wants the community and consumer to understand exactly what they're eating, which is why every species of fish is identified on the package.

Cofounder Aaron Longton says, "We think it's important to connect with the source of your food. By catching and processing your seafood ourselves, we knock out the corporate link in the supply chain and are able to tell the complete story of where your seafood comes from. We see ourselves as stewards of our environment; we care for it and it cares for us."

Panko-Crusted Steelhead Trout with Homemade Tartar Sauce

SERVES 4

Steelhead is a coastal rainbow trout that returns to fresh water to spawn after two or three years at sea. They look like salmon, are similar in taste to salmon, and can be found along the Pacific Ocean. They're considered a healthy fish with lean protein and contain more omega-3 than salmon. Most people remark that steelhead doesn't have the intensity of flavor that salmon has, and it's revered by many home cooks.

Steelhead can be prepared several different ways, but my family has always loved a good fish fry. So, when I find fresh steelhead, I like to crust it in panko, panfry it, and serve with my homemade tartar sauce.

For the Tartar Sauce

1 cup mayonnaise

⅓ cup dill pickle relish

1 tablespoon prepared horseradish

1 clove garlic, minced

1 tablespoon lightly chopped capers

1 tablespoon chopped fresh parsley

1 tablespoon chopped fresh dill

1 tablespoon fresh lemon juice

Dash of Worcestershire sauce

Salt and pepper, to taste

For the Trout

1½ pounds steelhead, cut into 4 pieces

½ teaspoon salt

½ teaspoon black pepper

¼ cup all-purpose flour

2 eggs

1 tablespoon Dijon mustard

1 teaspoon water

1 to 1½ cups panko bread crumbs

1 cup avocado oil, sunflower oil, or your favorite high-heat oil

Finishing salt

Lemon wedges, to serve

1. To prepare the tartar sauce, combine all the ingredients. Place it in a container and let it rest in the refrigerator for about 30 minutes prior to serving.

2. To prepare the fish, place the 4 fillets on a plate, pat dry with a paper towel, season each side with the salt and pepper, and dust each fillet with the flour.

3. Whisk the eggs with the Dijon mustard and water. Place the egg mixture in a shallow bowl. In another shallow bowl, add the panko bread crumbs.

continued . . .

4. Heat a large heavy-bottomed skillet over medium heat and add enough high-heat oil to cover the bottom of the skillet about 1 inch deep. This is panfrying without deep frying.

5. When the oil is hot, but not smoking, dip the flour-dusted fillets into the egg wash and then right into the panko, covering the entire surface of the fish. Gently place the panko-crusted fish into the hot oil. You will want to cook each side of the fish until they are golden brown. Depending on the thickness of the fish, this could take between 5 to 8 minutes total. As a rule, fish cooks 8 to 10 minutes for every inch of thickness. Steelhead can be ½ to 1 inch in thickness.

6. Once the fish is done, transfer it to a paper towel–lined plate. Sprinkle a little finishing salt on each fillet and serve with homemade tartar sauce and lemon wedges.

Side Dish Recommendations: Creamed Swiss Chard (page 111), Baked Summer Squash Tian (page 117), Carrot and Cilantro Salad with Ginger and Sun Butter Dressing (page 102), Layered Cornbread Salad with Spicy Avocado Ranch Dressing (page 94), Mexican Corn and Tomato Salad (page 97)

ABBEY CREEK VINEYARD

BERTONY FAUSTIN / NORTH PLAINS, OREGON

Brooklyn-born from Haitian immigrant parents, Bertony Faustin left the East Coast headed for California, with what he thought would be a brief stay in Oregon. However, he met the love of his life and decided to make Oregon home.

Although Bertony had a flourishing career in the medical profession, in 2007, after the passing of his father, he felt a complete life change was needed. This change would allow him to honor his father's memory and do something truly meaningful with his life. What Bertony decided to do next came as a surprise even to him.

Bertony purchased land from his wife's parents and the property happened to include 5 acres of grapes. While most of the property's neighbors were growing Christmas trees, Bertony said, "I'm going to make wine. And if that doesn't work, I'll make raisins."

This accidental farmer, award-winning documentary filmmaker of *Red, White, and Black,* and the first black winemaker in Oregon now makes some of the best wine in the Willamette Valley. Abbey Creek Vineyard's first vintage sold in 2008 and, in 2010, Abbey Creek wine won its first award.

Not long after the winery opened, Bertony realized that not everyone was going to be his customer. This gave him a sense of freedom to make wine his way—by letting Mother Nature do her job. He also realized he was in the people business. He wanted to create a place that was surrounded by good wine, community, connection, and conversation.

Abbey Creek Winery draws a diverse 200 visitors on any given weekend. One Friday evening every month, they host Art Night for the community and during the summer months they host long-table dinner events. Bertony says it's about breaking bread with our community, bridging gaps, and using wine as the tool.

While I was visiting, Bertony told me, "I'm inspired by the idea that you know how you come in the door, but it's up to me how you leave. It's the ability to create happiness and it empowers me to help and motivate others."

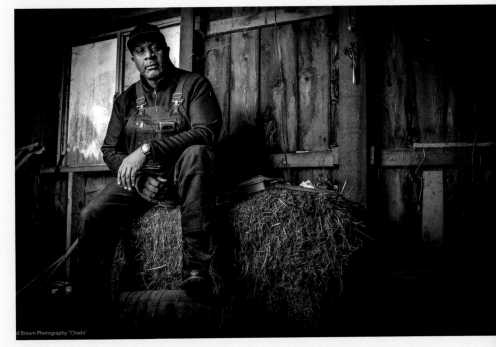

d Brown Photography "Chado"

One-Pan Fish Veronique (Pan-Cooked Fish with Grapes and Tarragon)

SERVES 4

Veronique is a classic French recipe that is typically prepared with fish (sometimes chicken) and garnished with the lightest white wine cream sauce and fresh grapes. You might think this recipe sounds fancy, but it couldn't be easier. It comes together quickly, so I recommend mise en place (having everything in its place).

Because Oregon is home to a variety of white fish, such as rockfish, cod, halibut, sole, and black cod, I use whatever is in season. I especially love to make this dish when I find fresh dover or petrale sole.

1 cup all-purpose flour

1 tablespoon dried tarragon

1½ to 2 pounds dover or petrale sole (or rockfish, cod, or halibut)

Salt and freshly ground black pepper

1 cup heavy cream

¼ cup chicken broth

2 to 4 tablespoons ghee

2 tablespoons unsalted butter

1 medium shallot, minced

2 cloves garlic, minced

½ cup white wine

½ to ¾ cup halved small green or red grapes, plus more for garnish, if desired

1 tablespoon chopped fresh tarragon

1. Mix together flour and dried tarragon. Pat down the fish with a paper towel and sprinkle the fish with salt and pepper on both sides.

2. In a small pan, mix together the heavy cream and chicken broth and warm over low heat. Take it off the heat to rest.

3. Heat a skillet on medium-high heat and add 2 tablespoons ghee. When the ghee is hot and slightly smoking, dredge the fish fillets through the flour and tarragon mixture and then dust off the excess.

4. Place the fillets in the hot ghee and pan-sear for 2 to 3 minutes on each side, depending on thickness, and until each side is golden. Transfer the pan-seared fillets to a platter and keep warm. Add additional ghee as needed to finish cooking the fish.

5. Cool the skillet enough to wipe it slightly with a paper towel, getting any burnt crisps out of the pan. Place the skillet back over medium heat and add the butter. When the butter is melted, add the shallot and cook until soft. Add garlic and sauté 1 minute longer.

6. Take the pan off the heat and stir in the white wine. Set the pan back over the heat and let the wine simmer for a minute or two, and then add the heavy cream mixture and grapes; let the sauce reduce by half.

7. Take the sauce off the heat and add the tarragon. Plate the fish fillets and ladle sauce over the fish, garnishing with extra grapes if desired. Serve immediately.

Side Dish Recommendations: Lemon-Herb Roasted New Potatoes (page 107), Roasted Green Bean Salad with Dried Cherries, Toasted Pine Nuts, and Goat Cheese (page 114), or Blackberry Burrata Salad (page 96)

Grilled Halibut with Blueberry Ginger Salsa

SERVES 4 TO 5

Oregon is home to one of the largest annual blueberry crops in the nation. It's a coveted season that arrives with anticipation and ends with a little sadness, unless I've squirreled away a stash in the freezer for a winter treat. Oregon blueberries can be found all summer season at most farms across the state and at farmers' markets, which is why I almost always have a steady flow of fresh summer blueberries on my kitchen counter from June to September.

Over the years, I've found that berries pair deliciously with savory ingredients, lending a subtle sweetness or tart flavor to a savory dish. I created this recipe several years ago when fresh blueberries were in season and I happened to have fresh halibut in the refrigerator. I didn't want to run to the market for extra ingredients, so I used what I had on hand. This combination of flavors did not disappoint. The salty essence of the fish combined with the sweetness of blueberries and savory aromatics of shallots and ginger worked deliciously together, creating a lovely, fresh, and flavorful meal.

If you can't find halibut, this salsa also pairs well with black cod, true cod, yellowfin tuna, or any other firm but flaky white fish. I recommend purchasing fish with skin on for grilling, and be sure you've got a well-oiled grill grate, or the fish will stick when it's flipped. A fish basket for the grill is a good alternative.

1½ to 2 pounds halibut, cut into 4 equal portions with skin on if available

2 tablespoons extra virgin olive oil

½ teaspoon salt

½ teaspoon black pepper

1 pint fresh blueberries, coarsely chopped

1 small to medium shallot, finely diced

1 teaspoon grated fresh ginger

2 tablespoons chopped fresh mint, plus more for garnish

Squeeze of lemon

Salt and pepper, to taste

1. Pat down the fish with a paper towel. Brush both sides of the fish pieces with 1 tablespoon olive oil and season with the salt and pepper.

2. In a medium bowl, gently toss together the blueberries, shallot, fresh ginger, chopped mint, remaining tablespoon olive oil, and lemon juice. Season to taste with salt and pepper. Let it sit at room temperature for about 30 minutes before serving. This will allow all those delicious flavors to meld together beautifully.

3. Preheat the grill to 400°F.

4. The key to grilling fish is a clean and well-oiled grate. It's much like using a cast-iron skillet—the more seasoned it is, the more nonstick it becomes. Once the grill has heated to 400°F, clean the grates and oil them several times.

5. Place the fish skin side down, close the lid, and grill for 2 to 4 minutes, or until the skin is crispy and browned. With a spatula, lift the fish to see if it comes off the grill easily. If it does, then it's ready to flip. If it doesn't, it may need another minute or two of cooking time. When the fish is ready, flip the fish to the other side and grill for another 2 to 4 minutes, or until the fish looks opaque or it's reached an internal temperature of 140°F. Most fish cooks 8 to 10 minutes for every inch of thickness.

6. Once the fish is done, transfer to a platter and top each fillet with a spoonful or two of salsa. Serve immediately.

Side Dish Recommendations: Lemon-Herb Roasted New Potatoes (page 107), Baked Summer Squash Tian (page 117), Oregon Shrimp Salad with Spicy Seafood Dressing (page 101)

Grilled Salmon Tacos with Pineapple Cilantro Slaw and Chipotle Lime Sauce

SERVES 4

I could eat tacos every night of the week, which is why this salmon taco recipe happened almost 15 years ago when salmon tacos weren't quite popular yet.

This recipe was my way of combining my love of tacos with the opportunity to score fresh salmon at the local fish market. Salmon is widely available here almost year-round, but it's truly best during salmon season when it's fresh from the water.

Over the years, these tacos have evolved through various adaptions. The addition of pineapple in this recipe, however, makes this version my favorite. If pineapple isn't your preference, substitute with diced mango or papaya.

For the Salmon

1½ pounds fresh salmon fillets

1 tablespoon avocado or olive oil

½ teaspoon chili powder

½ teaspoon ground cumin

½ teaspoon smoked paprika

½ teaspoon dried oregano

1 teaspoon salt

½ teaspoon black pepper

For the Chipotle Lime Sauce

¾ cup mayonnaise

1 tablespoon lime juice

Zest of 1 lime

1 to 2 chipotle chilis in adobo, depending on your spice preference

2 teaspoons granulated sugar

Black pepper (optional)

For the Pineapple Cilantro Slaw

2 cups shredded cabbage

½ cup fresh cilantro

¼ cup finely sliced green onions

¾ cup diced pineapple or more, to taste

8 to 10 corn tortillas, warmed or steamed

Lime wedges, fresh avocado slices, and salsa if desired, to serve

1. Heat the grill to 400°F.

2. Pat down the fish with paper towels and brush the fish with the oil. Then mix together the chili powder, cumin, smoked paprika, oregano, salt, and pepper. Sprinkle the mixture on the salmon. Let it sit while you prepare the sauce.

3. Prepare the sauce. In a food processor or blender, mix the mayonnaise, lime juice, lime zest, chipotle chilis, and sugar until smooth. Season with black pepper if desired. Reserve.

4. When the grill is hot, brush the grill grates with oil, place the salmon flesh side down, close the grill lid, and cook for 3 to 4 minutes. Open the grill lid and carefully flip the fish to the skin side down and grill for another 3 to 4 minutes, depending on thickness of the fish. The rule of thumb with fish: for every inch of thickness, cook it for 10 miinutes.

5. Once the salmon is done, transfer it to a platter. When the salmon has cooled slightly, flake the fish into bite-size pieces for the tacos. Remove any bones.

6. Prepare the slaw. Toss together the cabbage, cilantro, green onions, and diced pineapple.

7. To assemble, place some cabbage on the bottom of the corn tortilla, top with salmon, and then drizzle with sauce. Serve the tacos with additional lime wedges, fresh avocado, and salsa if desired.

Side Dish Recommendation: Mexican Corn and Tomato Salad (page 97)

Salmon Florentine

SERVES 4

We have five species of salmon here on the Pacific coast that migrate from ocean waters to fresh water to spawn. Salmon play an important role in the social and economic life of the Pacific Northwest. They are integral to our Native American history and extremely important to our regional ecology.

Oregon has taken great steps to preserve this precious resource, and although a few species of salmon aren't as easily found in markets due to preservation, we still have a beautiful supply of salmon to choose from.

Sockeye is most prevalent, and when it's fresh and in season, it cooks up tender, flaky, and flavorful. It's a smaller salmon when filleted, so it makes a perfect fish for baking, roasting, or quickly cooking on a hot grill.

I made this recipe after a visit to Abbey Creek Vineyard, just so I could pair it with their lush, balanced, and crisp Chardonnay. The salmon is nestled among sautéed spinach, onions, garlic, fresh herbs, heavy cream, and Parmesan, and pairs deliciously with the wine. The end result is a flavorful one-pan meal perfect for a busy weeknight or weekend dinner with friends.

2 tablespoons ghee

1 medium sweet onion, finely diced

3 cloves garlic, minced

1 tablespoon chopped fresh parsley

1 teaspoon chopped fresh thyme

1 tablespoon chopped fresh chives

6 to 8 ounces fresh baby spinach

1 cup heavy cream

¼ cup plus 2 tablespoons grated Parmesan

Zest of 1 lemon

Salt and pepper, to taste

1½ pounds salmon fillets, cut into 4 pieces

1 teaspoon Dijon mustard

2 tablespoons bread crumbs

1 tablespoon extra virgin olive oil

Squeeze of lemon, to serve

1. Preheat the oven to 375°F.

2. Add the ghee to an ovenproof skillet over medium heat. Add the onion and sauté until soft. Then stir in the garlic and herbs and cook 1 minute longer. Fold in the fresh spinach and toss until slightly wilted but not shriveled. If the heat is too high and the spinach begins to weep too much liquid, pour out the excess liquid before adding the heavy cream. Stir in the heavy cream and bring the cream to a lively simmer.

3. Stir in the ¼ cup grated Parmesan and lemon zest. Season to taste with salt and pepper. Remember that Parmesan can be salty, so don't over-salt the spinach.

4. Lightly season the salmon fillets with salt and pepper and then nestle the salmon into the spinach mixture. Mix together the remaining Parmesan, Dijon mustard, bread crumbs, and olive oil, and spread evenly over the salmon.

5. Bake in the oven 10 to 15 minutes. The rule of thumb with baking fish: for every inch of thickness, bake it for 10 minutes. Remove the skillet from the oven and squeeze fresh lemon over the salmon.

Side Dish Recommendations: Lemon-Herb Roasted New Potatoes (page 107), Baked Summer Squash Tian (page 117), Roasted Green Bean Salad with Dried Cherries, Toasted Pine Nuts, and Goat Cheese (page 114)

One-Pan Spicy Maple Chicken Thighs

SERVES 4

I'm sure I sound a bit *Portlandia*, but purchasing local chickens that led happy, healthy lives not only makes me a happy, healthy cook, but makes my recipes taste better. For this reason, I usually keep 3 to 4 frozen chickens and various packages of chicken thighs in my freezer at all times. This especially comes in handy when the weather cools and it's time to add this recipe to the dinner menu.

My daughters grew up dining on this quick chicken dinner and they look forward to it every fall and winter season. It can certainly be prepared year-round; however, the maple syrup makes it taste like a cool fall day.

I prefer chicken thighs, as they cook up tender most every time. The rich flavor of chicken thighs also complements the ingredients in this dish. I prepare this recipe in an ovenproof skillet, but it can also be finished in a baking dish.

1½ to 2 pounds (about 8) skinless, boneless chicken thighs

Salt and pepper

½ cup maple syrup

¼ cup Dijon mustard

1 tablespoon stone-ground mustard

2 teaspoons apple cider vinegar

2 tablespoons ghee or high-heat oil

½ cup diced onions

3 cloves garlic, minced

3 to 4 sprigs fresh thyme

Chopped fresh parsley, for garnish

1. Preheat the oven to 350°F.

2. Season the chicken thighs with salt and pepper.

3. Whisk together the maple syrup, Dijon mustard, stone-ground mustard, and vinegar.

4. Place an ovenproof skillet over medium-high heat and add the ghee. When the oil is hot, brown the chicken thighs and then transfer them to a plate. Don't cook through, as they will finish cooking in the oven.

5. Turn the heat down to medium. Add the diced onions to the skillet and cook the onions until softened, then add the garlic and thyme and cook 1 minute longer.

6. Remove the skillet from the heat and add the chicken back into the skillet with the onions and garlic. Or add the chicken thighs to a baking dish and top ith the onions and garlic. Pour the maple-mustard mixture over the chicken, moving the chicken pieces around to fully coat them in the sauce.

7. Place the skillet in the oven and bake for 25 to 30 minutes, or until the chicken is done—the internal temperature should be 160°F to 165°F.

8. Remove the skillet from the oven and let the chicken cool for 5 to 10 minutes. Garnish with parsley and serve.

Side Dish Recommendations: Winter Vegetable Gratin (page 108), Creamed Swiss Chard (page 111), Roasted Winter Beet Salad with Candied Nuts and Blue Cheese (page 93)

RED BIRD ACRES

LAURA AND ROBIN SAGE / CORVALLIS, OREGON

It is always a pleasure to walk the pastures of Red Bird Acres with farmers Laura and Robin Sage. I've been visiting their farm for several years now, and it never fails to delight my farm-girl heart.

I adore traipsing through the fields with a gaggle of piglets at my feet or several sows wandering nearby waiting for belly rubs. It turns out that pigs love belly rubs. Along with piglets, sows, and a docile boar or two, you'll find Red Freedom Ranger chickens, a flock of turkeys, and two large farm-and-flock guard dogs, Shasta and Lassen.

Laura and Robin Sage are first-generation farmers who started Red Bird Acres in 2013 in Corvallis, Oregon. As former outdoor educators who remain passionate about the environment and its inhabitants, they consider their farm to be first and foremost mission driven. "We believe in the importance of aligning our thoughts and actions: We began farming on the belief that it is necessary for environmental and human health to transition our agricultural system back to one based on small local economies where promoting human and animal health are at the forefront."

Laura and Robin are inspired by their passion for great food and take a holistic approach to farming that respects and fosters the health of the land and their animals. The farm utilizes a pasture-based rotational grazing system, and Red Bird Acres is one of only a handful of farms in Oregon that are Animal Welfare Approved by AGW (A Greener World).

You'll find Laura and Robin most spring, summer, and fall Saturdays at the Corvallis Farmers' Market as well as the Montavilla Farmers' Market in Portland and the Hillsboro Farmers' Market. They also have a CSA (community supported agriculture) for both chicken and pork products.

Slow-Braised Balsamic and Herb Chicken

SERVES 4

I've been making this recipe since 2013 after traveling to Tuscany and dining on some of the most amazing food. I adapted the original recipe a bit, however, to reflect our bounty here in Oregon. It's a lovely comfort meal of fresh herbs, locally raised chicken such as the succulent chicken I get from Red Bird Acres, and really good balsamic vinegar.

I love this served over creamy polenta, but it's equally delicious with mashed potatoes.

3 tablespoons ghee or avocado oil

8 bone-in, skinless chicken thighs or 4 chicken thigh quarters, or 1 whole chicken broken down into 6 to 8 pieces

Salt and pepper

1 large onion, halved and sliced

1 handful of at least three fresh herbs: rosemary, Italian parsley, oregano, thyme, and/or sage

4 cloves garlic, minced

¾ cup high-quality balsamic vinegar

¼ cup honey

¾ cup chicken broth

1 tablespoon tomato paste

Fresh chopped Italian parsley, for garnish

Mashed potatoes or creamy polenta, to serve

1. In a Dutch oven, heat the ghee over medium-high heat and season the chicken with salt and pepper. When the oil is hot, brown the chicken on both sides. Transfer chicken to a plate.

2. Turn down the heat to medium and add the onion and sauté until soft. Add the herbs and garlic and sauté 1 minute.

3. Mix together the balsamic vinegar, honey, chicken broth, and tomato paste. Place the chicken back into the Dutch oven and pour the balsamic vinegar mixture over the chicken. Cover and turn the heat to low or medium-low and simmer for 30 to 45 minutes, or until the chicken is done. Chicken should reach 165°F when done.

4. Remove the pot from the heat and then place the chicken on a platter. Strain the remaining sauce and pour it over the chicken. Garnish with the parsley. Serve over creamy polenta or mashed potatoes.

Note: To thicken the sauce, mix together 1 tablespoon cornstarch with 1 tablespoon cold water. Add this mixture to the strained sauce and bring to a boil. Simmer until thickened.

Beer-Braised Pork Roast with Garlic and Chive Mashed Potatoes

SERVES 6

There is something magical that happens when beer is used to braise meat, and my family has declared this method one of their favorite recipes. The pork is tender and flavorful and served with the most luscious sauce.

Lori Rice, my friend and author of the books *Food on Tap: Cooking with Craft Beer* and *Beer Bread*, says, "When beer is used to braise meats such as pork, it creates a rich, delicious sauce with deep flavors that complement the tender meat. The lower cooking temperature and longer cooking time really pulls the malty, sweet, toasted flavors from the beer. A standard lager can produce beautiful results, but an amber ale or brown ale are great options for stepping out of the box and creating more complex, creative flavors." I couldn't agree more. For extra Oregon flavor, test out some of the options from Rogue Ales of Newport, Oregon.

For the Pork Roast

- 3 to 4 pounds pork shoulder
- 1 teaspoon salt
- 1 teaspoon black pepper
- 1 tablespoon dried za'atar seasoning (see note below to make your own za'atar seasoning)
- 2 tablespoons high-heat oil (avocado, sunflower, ghee)
- 1 medium carrot, diced
- 2 ribs celery, diced
- 1 large sweet onion, diced
- 4 to 5 cloves garlic, finely diced
- One 4-inch stalk fresh rosemary
- 2 dried bay leaves
- 12 to 16 ounces beer, such as a lager, pilsner, amber, or brown ale

For the Garlic and Chive Mashed Potatoes

- 4 to 5 pounds Yukon Gold potatoes, cut into 2- to 3-inch cubes
- 1 tablespoon salt
- 6 cloves garlic
- 4 tablespoons (½ stick) unsalted butter
- 3 tablespoons cream cheese
- 1 cup heavy cream
- ¼ cup chopped fresh chives
- Salt and pepper, to taste
- Chopped fresh Italian parsley, for garnish

1. Preheat the oven to 350°F.

2. Cut the pork shoulder in half along the grain. You'll want two equally sized pieces, so they cook evenly. In a small bowl, mix together the salt, pepper, and za'atar seasoning. Rub the seasoning onto the pork.

3. In a Dutch oven, heat 1 tablespoon of oil over medium-high heat. When the oil is hot, brown both pieces of pork. Transfer the pork to a platter.

4. Add an additional tablespoon of oil if needed, and then stir in the carrots, celery, and onion. Sauté for 2 to 3 minutes, or until the vegetables are softened. Stir in the garlic and rosemary and cook 1 minute longer.

5. Place the pork back into the Dutch oven and then add bay leaves and pour in the beer. The beer should be half to three-quarters of the way up the side of the pork. Bring the liquid to a boil, place the lid on the Dutch oven, and cook in the oven for about 3 hours.

continued . . .

6. After 1 hour, turn the pork over and add additional beer if needed. Check it again after 2 hours, turning the pork once again. Check the pork for tenderness in 30 to 45 minutes. It should be fork tender. If not, let it cook another 15 to 20 minutes. Once the pork is done, remove it from the oven and let it rest for at least 15 minutes. The longer the pork rests, the more flavor it will develop.

7. While the pork is resting, make the mashed potatoes. Place the cubed potatoes in a pot and cover the potatoes with water. Add the salt and garlic to the water. Bring the water to a boil and then simmer for 12 to 15 minutes, or until potatoes are fork tender.

8. Drain the potatoes, keeping the garlic in the potatoes. Mash the potatoes lightly and then stir in butter, cream cheese, heavy cream, and chives. Season to taste with salt and pepper.

9. Place the pork on a platter and ladle the remaining sauce over the pork and garnish with the Italian parsley. Serve with the Garlic and Chive Mashed Potatoes.

Note: If you'd like more of an au jus–type sauce, strain the sauce into a bowl before pouring over the pork.

To make your own za'atar seasoning, combine 1 teaspoon ground cumin, 1 teaspoon powdered garlic, 1 teaspoon dried thyme, 1 teaspoon dried oregano, and 1 teaspoon toasted sesame seeds.

Side Dish Recommendations: Orange Marmalade and Miso Roasted Carrots with Toasted Sesame Seeds (page 105), Braised Red Cabbage with Apples and Bacon (page 104), Creamed Swiss Chard (page 111)

ROGUE ALES

NEWPORT, OREGON

One of the most iconic craft beer brands synonymous with the Pacific Northwest is Rogue Ales. Found in almost every location beer is sold, it has also become a beloved national brand and is distributed in more than 54 countries.

Quirky, playful, and possibly a bit rebellious, this brand has loads of charm and appeals to a variety of craft beer connoisseurs. From the well-known Rogue Ales signature brew, Dead Guy Ale, to cool and hip offerings such as the seasonal Santa's Private Reserve, a millennial-worthy Cold Brew IPA, and, one of my favorites, Yellow Snow Pilsner.

I had a chance to sample some of that beer right off the conveyor with Rogue Ales' Jim Cline, who showed me around Rogue Ales' brewery and world headquarters in Newport, Oregon. Rogue Ales' first brewpub opened in Ashland, Oregon, in 1988. A year later, Rogue Ales relocated to the quaint fishing town of Newport, Oregon. Today, there are nine brewpub and tasting room locations throughout the Pacific Northwest.

Thirty years later, with 300 nationwide employees, Rogue Ales is still brewing some of the best craft beer in the industry. If brewing beer and cider isn't enough, Rogue Ales branched out and built a distillery that makes whiskey, gin, rum, and vodka, along with a new line of sodas.

At Rogue Farms in Independence and Tygh Valley, Oregon, they grow more than a dozen ingredients for the beer, spirits, cider, and soda, along with several varieties of hops. They also have a few adorable pigs on hand and a tasting room with outdoor seating for those warm summer evenings.

Like many brands born and raised in Oregon, Rogue Ales continues to support its local communities with fundraisers and donations, and hosts a multitude of festive events and celebrations at each of the pub and tasting room locations.

Roasted Pork Tenderloin with Spiced Dried Plum Sauce

SERVES 4

I love a good sauce. Truly, it can make me giddy, which is why I have quite the repertoire of sauce recipes. When I was in culinary school, I'd come home each day and practice the techniques I learned. I'd make recipe after recipe and I served most of them with a sauce. One memorable evening, I created a recipe that did not have a sauce. I set the meal on the table and my daughter and husband gave me looks of bewilderment. I asked them why the funny faces and my daughter replied, "Where's the sauce?" Consequently, we almost always have a sauce with our dinner.

Sauces make my dinners easy, but they also add flavor and texture to a meal. This recipe is a perfect example: a simple roasted pork tenderloin cooked to juicy perfection and then served with a creamy and subtly spiced dried plum sauce. If you have other cuts of pork on hand, this sauce also pairs deliciously with pork loin and thin-cut pork chops.

1 teaspoon dried Italian herbs

1 teaspoon salt

½ teaspoon black pepper

1½ pounds pork tenderloin

1 tablespoon extra virgin olive oil

For the Spiced Plum Sauce

One 10-ounce package dried plums (prunes)

1½ cups dry white wine

1 cup heavy cream

¼ teaspoon ground cloves

¼ teaspoon ground cinnamon

1 heaping tablespoon red currant jelly or blackberry jelly

Salt and pepper, to taste

1 tablespoon chopped fresh Italian parsley, for garnish

1. Preheat the oven to 400°F.

2. Mix together the dried herbs, salt, and pepper. Place the tenderloin in a baking dish and rub with the olive oil. Sprinkle the dried herb-salt mixture on the entire tenderloin. Roast in the oven for 20 to 25 minutes, or until the internal temperature reaches 145°F.

3. Prepare the plum sauce. In a medium saucepan, add the plums and wine and heat over medium heat. Turn the heat down to low and let the wine and plums simmer uncovered until the wine has reduced by half, 8 to 10 minutes. Gently fold in the heavy cream, cloves, cinnamon, and red currant jelly.

4. Bring the sauce back to a gentle boil over medium heat. Then reduce the heat to a lively simmer until the sauce begins to thicken. The sauce will be done when it coats the back of a spoon. Season the sauce with salt and pepper to taste.

5. Once the pork is done, remove it from the oven and let it rest for 5 minutes. Slice the pork into thin slices and place on a platter. Drizzle the spiced plum sauce over the pork and garnish with the Italian parsley. Serve immediately.

Side Dish Recommendations: Shaved Brussels Sprouts Salad with Winter Squash, Dried Cherries, and Bacon with Maple Vinaigrette (page 91), Orange Marmalade and Miso Roasted Carrots with Toasted Sesame Seeds (page 105), Oregon Shrimp Salad with Spicy Seafood Dressing (page 101)

CODY WOOD, FARMER

JUNCTION CITY, OREGON

I've toured Cody Wood's sheep farm twice in the last three years, and every time it's an adventure. Whether I'm hanging on for dear life while sitting on the back of a speeding four-wheeler, trying to capture the perfect farm shot, or watching Cody's prized border collies work their magic herding sheep, I always find myself smiling as I leave the farm.

During my first farm visit with Cody, he told me that sheep farming is something he always knew he wanted to do. It just seems to be second nature to Cody.

Cody has been sheep farming in Junction City, Oregon, and the surrounding Willamette Valley for ten years. He learned the artistry of sheep farming while spending time in New Zealand many years ago. Once Cody returned to Oregon, he put everything he learned into action. As time passed, he realized he needed to learn the craft of meat-cutting and eventually found himself training with some of the best meat-cutting professionals in New York City.

This is classic Cody Wood. He sees a need and then determines the best way to solve it. Through education and research, Cody is constantly working to make new and innovative advancements in the world of farming. His love of the land and the work is evident when listening to him explain the complexities of raising sheep on the healthiest land possible.

Today, Cody continues to raise sheep in Oregon for several co-ops as well as Cattail Creek Lamb, and recently started raising cattle in northern California. You can follow Cody and his three tack-smart border collies—Beef, Brooklyn, and Brit—working sheep and cattle on his Instagram page.

Salisbury-Style Meatloaf with Beef Broth Gravy

SERVES 6

Salisbury steak and gravy was a regular dish on my childhood family table, and it was truly loved by my bright-eyed character of a grandfather. If I had to guess, I'd say it was his favorite. He used to refer to this fancy pan-cooked hamburger as his "steak and gravy," which always made me laugh.

Years later, I found myself recreating this tasty dish and making it into a meatloaf with a rich beef broth gravy. It works well when I'm feeding a crowd and it makes a lovely Sunday dinner. It also makes the best leftover grilled cheese and meatloaf sandwiches.

For the Meatloaf

3 slices stale or dry bread, or ⅓ cup bread crumbs

⅓ cup warm milk

2 tablespoons ghee, avocado oil, or extra virgin olive oil

1 large yellow onion, diced

3 cloves garlic, minced

1½ pounds ground beef

1 tablespoon chopped fresh parsley

1½ teaspoons salt

1 teaspoon black pepper

1 tablespoon Worcestershire sauce

2 eggs, lightly whisked

For the Beef Broth Gravy

2 tablespoons unsalted butter

2 tablespoons all-purpose flour

2 cups beef broth

Salt and pepper, to taste

1 tablespoon chopped fresh parsley, for garnish

1. Preheat the oven to 375°F.

2. In a food processor, add the bread and pulse until the bread is reduced to fine crumbles. Add the bread crumbs to the warm milk. Stir and then let them sit.

3. In a skillet, heat ghee over medium heat. Add the onion and cook until nicely golden brown. Add garlic and stir 1 minute longer. Take the pan off the heat.

4. Place the ground beef in a large bowl and then pour the onions and garlic over the meat. Add parsley, salt, pepper, Worcestershire sauce, soaked bread crumbs, and eggs. Gently stir to combine.

5. Turn the meat onto a parchment paper–lined baking sheet and form a rectangular loaf, 10-by-5 inches. Place the baking sheet in the oven and bake the meatloaf for 45 minutes to 1 hour.

6. While the meatloaf is baking, make the gravy. Add butter to a medium skillet over medium heat. When the butter is melted, stir in the flour. Slowly whisk in the beef broth and continue to whisk over medium heat until the gravy has thickened. Season to taste with salt and pepper.

7. When the meatloaf is done, let it cool for about 10 minutes. Slice and place the slices on a platter and drizzle with a little of the gravy. Garnish with the parsley.

Side Dish Recommendations: Lemon-Herb Roasted New Potatoes (page 107), Layered Cornbread Salad with Spicy Avocado Ranch Dressing (page 96), Mexican Corn and Tomato Salad (page 97)

Braised Lamb Shanks with Five Spice and Pinot Noir

SERVES 6

I love it when farmer friends are in the neighborhood and drop by with farm-fresh ingredients. This is exactly what farmer Cody Wood did when he visited my town. Cody raises sheep all over the Willamette Valley and on this occasion, he brought us the most beautiful cuts of lamb shank. So, of course, a lamb shank recipe had to happen. I like to call this recipe elevated comfort food. It's a succulent and flavorful dish that is fairly easy to prepare and then it just hangs out in the oven and becomes tender and luscious.

I serve these gorgeous slow-braised lamb shanks over garlic mashed potatoes or creamy polenta, but they would be equally lovely with mashed sweet potatoes, butternut squash, or mashed cauliflower.

Salt and pepper

6 lamb shanks (about 1 pound each)

2 to 3 tablespoons ghee or high-heat oil

2 carrots, diced

2 medium to large onions, diced

6 to 8 cloves garlic, minced

Three 4-inch sprigs fresh thyme

1 tablespoon fresh chopped parsley

1 tablespoon five spice powder (see note below to make your own five spice powder)

1 to 2 dried bay leaves

One 28-ounce can whole tomatoes

1 bottle Pinot Noir, minus one 4-ounce glass for the cook!

1 to 2 cups beef broth

1 tablespoon cornstarch

1 tablespoon cold water

Chopped fresh parsley, for garnish

1. Preheat the oven to 325°F.

2. Salt and pepper the lamb shanks. Heat the ghee in a Dutch oven or ovenproof pot over medium-high heat. When the oil is hot, brown the lamb shanks on all sides. You may need to brown the shanks two or three at a time to avoid overcrowding the pot. Overcrowding will prevent a good browning on the meat. Transfer the lamb shanks to a platter and reserve.

3. Turn down the heat to medium and add the carrots and onions to the pot. Cook until they are slightly soft, 2 to 3 minutes. Stir in the garlic, thyme, and fresh parsley. Cook for 1 minute longer.

4. Stir in the five spice powder, bay leaves, tomatoes, Pinot Noir, and 1 cup beef broth. Nestle the lamb shanks along with any juices accumulated into the pot. If the lamb shanks are not covered by the liquid, add enough beef stock to just cover the shanks.

5. Bring the liquid to a boil and then take the pot off the heat, cover with a tight-fitting lid, and place it in the center rack in the oven.

6. Braise the shanks for 2 hours covered, checking the shanks every 45 minutes to be sure there is still enough liquid in the pot. If the liquid is evaporating too quickly, add additional beef broth or water. Then remove the lid and braise an additional 30 minutes uncovered.

7. When the shanks are done, the meat will be fork tender. Transfer the shanks to a platter and keep warm.

8. Mix together the cornstarch and cold water to make a slurry. Place the pot with the remaining sauce over medium high heat and bring it to a slow boil. Stir in the slurry and continue to simmer until the sauce begins to thicken.

9. To serve, ladle some of the sauce, either with vegetables or strained, over the lamb shanks and garnish with the parsley. Serve the lamb shanks with a side of the remaining sauce.

Note: To make five spice powder, mix together 3 tablespoons cinnamon, 5 star anise, 1½ teaspoons fennel seeds, 1½ teaspoons black peppercorns, and ½ teaspoon ground cloves. Add the mixture to a spice blender or spice mill and blend until finely ground. Keep in an airtight container for up to 3 months. Makes about ¼ cup.

Side Dish Recommendations: Lemon-Herb Roasted New Potatoes (page 107), Creamed Swiss Chard (page 111), Blackberry Burrata Salad (page 96)

Ground Beef and Sausage Pub Burger with Sautéed Onions and Special Sauce

MAKES 6 BURGERS

Drive anywhere in Oregon and you'll find the best selection of homemade sausage. We have a plethora of sausage here that I use to create all sorts of delicious dishes, such as this pub burger that I created several years ago using a local sweet Italian sausage.

Locally sourced ground beef is combined with farm-fresh ground sausage and then layered with aromatics and a little spice just for fun. It's grilled and topped with sautéed sweet onions and my special sauce. I serve it on sweet Hawaiian bread buns for the ultimate burger.

For the Special Sauce

1 cup mayonnaise

¼ cup chili sauce

1 clove garlic, minced

1 teaspoon lemon juice

1 teaspoon Cajun seasoning

¼ cup finely chopped green onions

1 teaspoon prepared horseradish

1 teaspoon Worcestershire sauce

1 tablespoon chopped fresh parsley

Dash of hot sauce (optional)

For the Sautéed Onions

2 tablespoons unsalted butter

1 large sweet onion, halved and thinly sliced

½ teaspoon salt

For the Burger

1 pound ground beef

½ pound ground sweet Italian sausage

1 to 2 teaspoons Cajun or Creole Seasoning (depending on how spicy the sausage is)

2 green onions, finely chopped or minced

1 to 2 cloves garlic, minced

1 tablespoon Worcestershire sauce

1 tablespoon prepared horseradish

½ cup panko bread crumbs

¼ cup warmed whole milk

Olive oil or vegetable oil, for brushing

Salt and pepper

6 Hawaiian sweet buns or potato buns (the sweet buns taste amazing with this burger)

6 tomato slices

6 fresh lettuce leaves

1. Prepare the sauce. In a small bowl, combine all ingredients. Set aside.

2. Prepare the sautéed sweet onions. In a sauté pan over medium-low heat, add the butter. When the butter is melted, add the sliced sweet onion. Sauté the onion until golden brown and slightly caramelized. Take off the heat and season with salt.

3. Prepare the burgers. In a large bowl, gently combine the ground beef and the ground Italian sausage. Add the seasoning, green onions, garlic, Worcestershire sauce, and horseradish and gently combine. Don't overwork the meat.

4. Add the panko bread crumbs to a bowl and mix in the warm milk. Mix this into the burger meat until well distributed, but, again, be careful not to overwork the mixture or else the burgers will be tough.

5. Preheat the grill to 400°F. Make six hamburger patties and then brush them with olive oil. Sprinkle with a little salt and pepper. Place the patties on the grill and cook for 3 to 4 minutes each side for medium or 5 to 6 minutes each side for well done.

You should see nice grill marks or nicely browned color on each side. I like to cook my burgers to medium at 160°F to 165°F internal temperature.

6. Once the burgers are done, let them rest for 5 minutes. Assemble the burgers by adding special sauce to both halves of the bun and placing the burger on the bottom half of the bun. Top the burger with sautéed onions, then the tomato slice and let-tuce. Place the top half of the bun on top of the let-tuce and serve. Enjoy!

Side Dish Recommendations: Mexican Corn and Tomato Salad (page 97), Carrot and Cilantro Salad with Ginger and Sun Butter Dressing (page 102), Blackberry Burrata Salad (page 96)

FISHER RIDGE FARM

SUE AND RALPH FISHER / SUBLIMITY, OREGON

I met Sue Fisher early one evening at their family farm expecting a brief visit, but instead, she graciously invited me to tag along while she completed the evening chores. I was thrilled at the chance to follow along and immerse myself in farm life, if only for a few hours.

Located on the rolling Waldo Hills, the historic Fisher Ridge Farm features dramatic views overlooking the Willamette Valley. The Pudding River meanders through the stunning 300-acre farm, Suffolk sheep graze, chickens roam, piglets romp in the mud, and happy farm dogs guard the flock. On land not far from the farmhouse, Ralph and Sue Fisher raise nearly 80 head of Simmental-cross cattle on some of the most beautiful and pristine pastures.

Fisher Ridge Farm began in 1879 when Ralph Fisher's great-great-grandparents, Joseph and Theresa Fisher, settled here via Wisconsin from Bohemia. Today, the Fisher Family have had seven generations on this farm, including their four children and six grandchildren.

Ralph and Sue have worked tirelessly over the last 40 years to raise healthy livestock on quality pasture, using wheat, oats, and flax that they grow themselves.

None of their animals are fed corn or soy, nor do they receive any growth enhancement. They're happy animals grazing on lush pasture. Ralph and Sue believe this is the best way to raise their livestock, and it gives the consumer the ability to buy their meat with confidence in superior, healthy, and flavorful food.

You can find Fisher Ridge Farms meat and poultry at the Oregon City and Silverton Farmers' Markets or order a build-a-box through their Facebook page.

Sunday Beef Pot Roast with Creamy Parmesan Polenta

SERVES 6

According to my daughters, our Sunday dinners have always been the best meal of the week. This sentiment makes me smile. I'd like to believe this recipe had something to do with it.

It's one of the first meals I make as soon as the weather begins to cool. This dish is a simple slow-braised recipe that begins with bacon and a quality cut of beef from farms such as Fisher Ridge Farm in Sublimity, Oregon, and involves flavorful aromatics, herbs, and Oregon wine. The finished dish is served over the creamiest yellow polenta for the ultimate Sunday pot roast.

For the Pot Roast

4 pounds beef top rump or top-side roast

Salt and pepper

6 slices bacon, chopped

1 large yellow onion, diced

2 ribs celery, diced

2 medium carrots, diced

8 cloves garlic, sliced thin

1 teaspoon freshly cracked black pepper

2 cups dry red wine (I use an Oregon Pinot Noir)

One 28-ounce can whole tomatoes with liquid

1 teaspoon dried rosemary, crushed, or one 4-inch stalk fresh rosemary

½ teaspoon dried thyme, or one 3-inch sprig fresh thyme

1 tablespoon chopped fresh Italian parsley, plus more for garnish

1 teaspoon salt (optional)

For the Creamy Parmesan Polenta

3 cups whole milk

½ cup quick-cook polenta

¼ cup grated Parmesan

Salt and pepper, to taste

1. Season the roast with salt and pepper on all sides and preheat the oven to 350°F.

2. In an ovenproof Dutch oven or heavy stockpot on medium-high heat, brown the roast on all sides. Transfer the browned roast to a plate and set aside.

3. Turn the heat to medium and add the chopped bacon. Brown the bacon until slightly crisp and then add the onion, celery, and carrots. Cook the veggies until soft and then add the garlic. Cook for 1 minute.

4. Sprinkle the veggies with the teaspoon of pepper and then add the wine, scraping the browned bits off the bottom of the pot. Let the wine simmer for a minute or two. Slightly crush the tomatoes by hand or with a fork and stir in the tomatoes.

continued . . .

5. Add the dried herbs and chopped fresh Italian parsley and combine with the veggie mixture. Let the mixture come to a slow boil and then place the beef back into the pot.

6. Turn off the stovetop, put the lid on the pot, and place the pot in the preheated oven. Cook for 4 to 5 hours in the oven until the beef falls apart. Check for seasoning, adding the teaspoon of salt if needed.

7. Prepare the polenta. In a medium stockpot, heat the milk on medium. Stir every once and a while so the milk won't burn on the bottom. When the milk comes to a slow boil, add the polenta and stir.

8. Continue stirring the polenta until it thickens to a heavy creamy texture. Take it off the heat and stir in the Parmesan. Season with salt and pepper to taste.

9. Before the polenta sets, pour it onto a serving dish. Place pieces of the roast over the polenta and ladle the remaining sauce over the beef. Garnish with additional chopped Italian parsley and serve.

Note: Use whole tomatoes in this recipe rather than crushed tomatoes. Canned crushed tomatoes are actually the end bits of the tomatoes and don't have quite as much flavor as the whole canned tomatoes.

Side Dish Recommendations: Orange Marmalade and Miso Roasted Carrots with Toasted Sesame Seeds (page 105), Braised Red Cabbage with Apples and Bacon (page 104)

Grilled Flank Steak with Sautéed Blueberries, Shallots, and Blue Cheese

SERVES 6

It seems every summer I end up with several flats of Oregon fruit and berries on my kitchen counter as well as fresh, flavorful flank steak from our local farms. One particular summer I had blueberries that needed to be used or turned into jam before they expired, or before the fruit flies invaded.

I decided to sauté the fresh blueberries with shallots and garlic that I had just procured from the farmers' market, and then sprinkled the savory berry mixture over our grilled flank steak and garnished the entire dish with Rogue Creamery blue cheese. It was such a huge hit with my family, the recipe is now a summer staple.

2½ to 3 pounds flank steak, pounded out to ½ to 1 inch thick with a meat mallet

1 tablespoon extra virgin olive oil

½ teaspoon garlic powder

½ teaspoon onion powder

1 teaspoon smoked paprika

1 teaspoon salt

½ teaspoon ground black pepper

2 tablespoons ghee, 1 tablespoon butter, or 1 tablespoon extra virgin olive oil

¼ cup finely diced shallots (about 1 small to medium shallot)

2 cups fresh blueberries

1 clove garlic, minced

¼ cup thinly sliced green onions

Salt and pepper, to taste

4 ounces crumbled Rogue Creamery blue cheese

¼ cup fresh cilantro

1. Preheat the grill to 425°F.

2. Brush the flank steak with the olive oil. In a small bowl, mix together the garlic powder, onion powder, smoked paprika, salt, and pepper. Then sprinkle the mixture on both sides of the flank steak.

3. Once the grill is hot, place the flank steak on the grill and cook for 5 to 7 minutes on each side, for medium rare. I typically cook my flank steak to 130°F to 135°F internal temperature.

4. Once the steak is done, transfer it to a platter and let it rest. While the steak is resting, heat the ghee in a sauté pan over medium heat. When the ghee is hot and melted, add the diced shallots and let them cook for about 1 minute.

5. Stir in the blueberries and garlic and sauté for 1 to 2 minutes longer. Take the pan off the heat and add the green onions. Season to taste with the salt and pepper.

6. Transfer the steak to a cutting board and slice the flank steak thinly against the grain. This will ensure a more tender bite. Place the steak on a platter, and then pour the blueberry mixture over the steak and garnish with crumbled blue cheese and cilantro. Serve immediately.

Side Dish Recommendations: Lemon-Herb Roasted New Potatoes (page 107), Baked Summer Squash Tian (page 117), Mexican Corn and Tomato Salad (page 97)

ROGUE CREAMERY AND DAIRY

CENTRAL POINT, OREGON

Southern Oregon is home to the award-winning Rogue Creamery, which creates some of the most exquisite handmade cheeses in the world. Their cheese begins with healthy, happy cows grazing on flavorful local grasses at their dairy farm located in the Rogue Valley. The pastures are plentiful in nutrients, which makes the milk flavorful, rich in protein and butterfat, and ideal for producing Rogue's award-winning cheeses.

We had the opportunity to tour the charming dairy farm with Dairy Manager Zach Rose and Marketing Manager Marguerite Merritt one cool spring morning. The dairy farm features 68 certified organic grazing acres of cloves, orchard grass, and native fescue along with one of the few AMS (automatic milking systems) in Oregon.

A few miles down the road from the dairy farm is Rogue Creamery, located in Central Point, Oregon. There, we toured the delightful cheese shop, tasting room, and creamery campus with our informative guide, Craig Nelson. In the cheese shop, visitors can watch some of the behind-the-scenes cheesemaking techniques, and you don't want to miss a visit to the small sandwich shop that makes a delectable Grilled Rogue Cheese Sandwich.

Rogue Creamery has been inspired by a sense of place for 80 years. It draws from the beauty and flavors of southern Oregon's Rogue River Valley to create handcrafted blue cheese, Cheddar, and TouVelle. It is dedicated to holistic, organic, and sustainable practices that create the most delicious cheeses. Craig Nelson says, "Producing Rogue cheese is a meticulous process and one that is dedicated to sustainability, service, and the art and tradition of creating the world's finest organic handmade cheese."

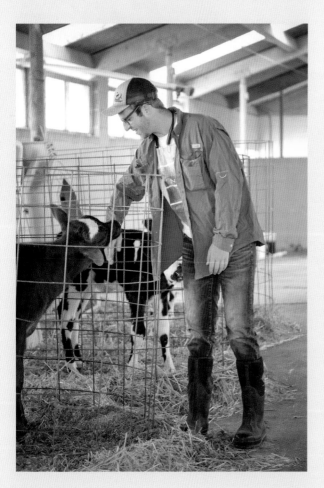

DESSERTS

Cherry Pandowdy

SERVES 8

Cherry season in Oregon always seems to sneak up on me. It arrives like a subtle breeze and then, before you know it, leaves like a brisk wind. So, when it does arrive, my family tries to make the most of it. This fun and simple recipe is perfect for a weekend barbecue, and I've been known to eat it for breakfast.

If you've never heard the term "pandowdy," it simply means it's a dessert baked in a pan and topped with little pieces of pie dough or puff pastry. When it's done, it looks a little dowdy. It's a pandowdy.

2 pounds pitted cherries

Zest and juice of 1 orange

1 cup granulated sugar

Pinch of salt

3 tablespoons quick-cooking tapioca

1 sheet puff pastry, completely thawed and cut into
    nine 3-inch squares

1 tablespoon coarse sugar (optional)

1 egg

1 teaspoon water

Vanilla bean ice cream or brandied whipped cream,
    to serve

1. Preheat the oven to 425°F.

2. Mix together the cherries, orange zest, orange juice, sugar, salt, and quick-cooking tapioca. Let the filling sit for at least 15 to 30 minutes prior to baking.

3. Place the filling in an 8-by-11-inch or 9-by-11-inch baking dish. Then place each puff pastry square over the top of the cherry filling. This is where you can get artistic. Sometimes I just place the squares to overlap at different angles and sometimes I keep them fairly uniform. Just have fun—it's a pandowdy!

4. In a small bowl, whisk the egg and water. Brush the egg wash over the puff pastry and sprinkle with coarse sugar if desired. Place the baking pan in the oven and bake for 25 to 30 minutes, or until the filling is bubbling and the top is golden brown.

5. Allow the pandowdy to cool before serving. Serve with vanilla bean ice cream or a brandied whipped cream.

HOOD RIVER LAVENDER FARMS

ODELL, OREGON

ucts such as handmade lavender soap, aromatherapy items, and essential lavender oils and products made with steam-distilled certified organic lavender. They also have a line of culinary lavender and dried lavender products for the home.

Every July, Hood River Lavender Farms hosts the annual Lavender Daze, which is a local lavender festival in the Columbia River Gorge. The farm, as well as the festival, is family- and dog-friendly. The festival features special events, art, food, and of course, all things lavender.

Hood River Lavender Farms just outside of Hood River, Oregon, is one of the most visually stunning farms in the Columbia River Gorge. Fields of lavender dot the landscape while views of Mount Hood and Mount Adams grace the skyline. This is an enchanting farm that never ceases to thrill my lavender-loving heart.

Open from April to October, Hood River Lavender Farms operates a U-pick program with over 80 varieties of lavender. There is ample room for visitors to stroll or sit among the lavender, take a walk through the wildflower garden, or languish under a tent while sipping lavender lemonade or enjoying the famous lavender ice cream.

There is a small store filled with lavender prod-

Strawberries in Brandied Cream

SERVES 4 TO 6

When I was young, my mom would place a bowl of brown sugar, a bowl of sour cream, and a bowl of whole strawberries on the table. We'd dip the strawberries in the sour cream and then roll them in brown sugar and pop them in our mouths with squeals of delight.

I've created a grown-up version of that recipe. This is one of my favorite ways to serve farm-fresh Oregon strawberries. It is fun, festive, tasty, and it can still make me squeal with delight. Of course, you can always omit the brandy for a child-friendly version and it'll still taste delicious.

1 cup crème fraîche

½ cup cream cheese, softened

¼ cup brown sugar

2 to 3 tablespoons brandy

1 quart strawberries, washed, trimmed, and sliced

Fresh sprigs of mint, for garnish

1. In the bowl of an electric mixer, add the crème fraîche, cream cheese, brown sugar, and brandy. Blend until smooth.

2. Divide strawberries among four to six dessert glasses, martini glasses, or small dessert bowls and then dollop with the brandied cream. Garnish with fresh sprigs of mint.

Blueberry Lavender Crumble

SERVES 4 TO 6

I always look forward to the summer U-pick season in Oregon, especially when it involves a day spent at Hood River Lavender Farms. Inevitably, I come home with beautiful bouquets of fresh lavender to dry, along with an assortment of lavender creams, soaps, and, of course, culinary lavender.

This recipe is quick to assemble, deliciously fragrant, wheat-free, and can feed a crowd. Although I've written this recipe to serve 4 to 6, it can easily be doubled using a larger baking dish.

If you'd like to make a larger batch of the Lavender Sugar to keep on hand, you can find the recipe on page 15.

½ cup granulated sugar

1 tablespoon dried culinary lavender

3 cups fresh blueberries

1 tablespoon cornstarch

1 cup almond flour

½ cup rolled oats

½ teaspoon salt

8 tablespoons (1 stick) unsalted butter, melted

Vanilla ice cream, to serve (optional)

1. Preheat the oven to 350°F.

2. Place the sugar and dried lavender in a food processor and blend until the lavender is infused into the sugar. Or, using a mortar and pestle, grind the lavender into the sugar until infused.

3. In a bowl, mix the blueberries with cornstarch. Place the blueberries into the bottom of an 8-inch square baking dish. Sprinkle ¼ cup of the lavender sugar over the top of the blueberries.

4. In a medium bowl, mix together the almond flour, oats, salt, and the remaining ¼ cup of lavender sugar. Then mix in ¼ cup of melted butter until you have crumbles.

5. Spread almond flour crumbles over the top and then drizzle with the additional ¼ cup butter.

6. Place the dish in the oven and bake for about 30 minutes or until the sides of the crumble are bubbly and the top is golden brown.

7. Remove from the oven and let it cool for about 10 minutes before serving. This crumble is lovely on its own or served with vanilla ice cream.

Mixed Berry Gratin

SERVES 4

Berry farms, such as Hoffman Farms Store in Scholls, Oregon, dot our serene valley landscape. Because berries grow in abundance here, it seems they find their way into every meal of the day, especially during the summer months.

I love to make this recipe during the summer when berries are fresh, but it will work with frozen berries as well. I serve this as a light and slightly sweet dessert, but I've also served this for brunch. I use crème brûlée ramekins, as I find this not only perfectly portions the gratin, but offers a lovely presentation. This is definitely one of those simple recipes that allows our cherished Oregon berries to shine.

1 tablespoon unsalted butter

2 cups fresh assorted berries

1½ cups plain or vanilla Greek yogurt or crème fraîche

½ cup dark brown sugar

¼ cup finely chopped almonds or crumbled vanilla cookies, for garnish

1. Preheat the oven to the low broil setting.

2. Butter each ramekin and then place the ramekins on a baking sheet. Divide the berries among the ramekins and then dollop a few tablespoons of yogurt on the berries. Top the yogurt and berries with a few tablespoons of dark brown sugar.

3. Place the baking sheet on the center rack in the oven. Broil the gratins just until the berries are warm and the brown sugar is caramelized, 5 to 10 minutes. Garnish with chopped nuts or crumbled cookies. Serve warm.

HOFFMAN FARMS STORE

JAY AND KELLY HOFFMAN / SCHOLLS, OREGON

This is one of those farms where I could spend the entire day roaming the berry fields picking berries, snacking on berry shakes or homemade berry pie, and enjoying the stunning valley views. Hoffman Farms Store has created a magical farm experience for children and adults alike, and it's a destination not to be missed.

Just outside Portland in Scholls, Oregon, Hoffman Farms Store is a vision that Jay and Kelly Hoffman dreamed up when their children were still young. "Jay and Kelly dreamed of building a legacy in the Scholls community," according to one of the (now-grown) Hoffman children, "where other families could step into a world of our family farm and enjoy the fruits of our collective labor." Today, all three of the Hoffman children—Melissa, Korina, and Jayson—are involved in working the farm and are deeply committed to the community in which they live. They work to create a space for the community to gather with family and friends to celebrate new memories together.

Throughout the summer, they grow a variety of berries—strawberries, blueberries, raspberries, blackberries, marionberries, and tayberries—for U-pick as well as for purchase in the farm store. Also found in the farm store are their original freshly baked pies, jams, jellies, and more.

The farm is complete with a wedding venue, on-farm bakery, and barbecue truck. There is also a large children's play structure and a train that travels the property and makes stops at the strawberry field in the summer and the pumpkin patch in the fall, along with space to linger, eat, and enjoy the day.

BOB'S RED MILL NATURAL FOODS

BOB MOORE, FOUNDER / MILWAUKEE, OREGON

Bob's Red Mill website says, "Before you get to know our business, you need to meet the man behind it—Bob Moore. You'll recognize his friendly face on our products, and if you ever visit our mill, Whole Grains Store, or Visitor's Center, you might even get to meet the man himself." Well, I had the great privilege of meeting the man himself at company headquarters in Milwaukie, Oregon.

Bob Moore's story is as inspirational and as diverse as his product line. To truly give readers a glimpse of his career, I'd have to write an entire book. Luckily, someone has already done this. The long and short of it is, Bob attributes his career success in whole grain to his wife, Charlee.

He and Charlee met on a blind date in 1952 and, not long after, Charlee became inspired by healthy eating and began cooking with whole grain. Charlee spent time researching the health and nutritional benefits of whole grain, and fast-forward 27 years, Bob's Red Mill was born.

Today, Bob's Red Mill Natural Foods is a household name and produces more than 400 different whole grain and gluten-free products. And while the products are recognizable, so is the icon. I found Bob to be genuinely passionate about health, nutrition,

and building a company based on generosity and hard work.

I asked Bob what inspires him. His reply: "the golden rule." In other words, treat others as you want to be treated. Bob lives by this mantra every day and has shown it by giving back to his community, funding nutrition-based research, and monthly profit sharing with his employees. Bob is proud to have made Bob's Red Mill into an employee-owned company.

When I asked Bob which product was his favorite, he replied, "The steel cut oats. You just can't beat a bowl of creamy Bob's Red Mill steel cut oats." I'd have to agree.

Peach Upside-Down Ginger Cake

SERVES 8

This cake recipe has been on my dessert menu for years. It's an adaption of my mom's Pineapple Upside-Down Cake, which always seemed to have a permanent place on the kitchen counter. It's an easy cake to prepare and it's perfect for a last-minute dessert or as a brunch cake.

I've adapted this recipe using fresh Oregon peaches instead of the traditional pineapple. I also added ground ginger to the cake batter, creating a sweet, slightly spicy and moist cake. I love to serve this cake with whipped cream, and in the summer, I pair it with vanilla bean ice cream and caramel sauce.

8 tablespoons (1 stick) unsalted butter, melted
   or at room temperature, plus an additional
   2 tablespoons melted

¼ cup brown sugar

2 tablespoons maple syrup (optional)

4 to 5 cups sliced peaches (4 to 5 medium to large
   fresh peaches)

2 cups all-purpose flour

1 teaspoon baking powder

1 teaspoon baking soda

¼ teaspoon salt

1½ teaspoons ground ginger

¾ cup granulated sugar

1 large egg

1 teaspoon vanilla extract

1 cup buttermilk

Fresh whipped cream or vanilla bean ice cream,
   to serve

1. Preheat the oven to 350°F.

2. Place the 2 tablespoons of melted butter into the bottom of a 9-inch-round baking pan or a 9-by-11-inch baking dish. Sprinkle with brown sugar and drizzle with maple syrup if desired.

3. Place the peach slices in a circular pattern on top of the butter and sugar.

4. Whisk together flour, baking powder, baking soda, salt, and ground ginger. In a stand mixer or another bowl, mix together the 8 tablespoons of butter and sugar until nicely combined. Stir in the egg until mixture looks creamy.

5. Stir in vanilla extract and buttermilk. Mix the dry ingredients into the wet ingredients until well combined.

6. Pour the batter over the peaches and then place the baking pan in the oven and bake for 40 to 50 minutes, or until the cake is firm to the touch or a knife comes out clean.

7. Take the cake out of the oven and let it cool for 10 to 15 minutes. Then flip the cake onto a cake platter or cake plate. If any peaches fall off while flipping, just place them back onto the cake.

8. Serve this gorgeous summer cake with fresh whipped cream or vanilla bean ice cream.

Note: If you don't have buttermilk, you can easily make it with 1 cup whole milk minus 1 tablespoon, combined with 1 tablespoon white vinegar. Stir and let sit for about 5 minutes.

Baked Raspberry Lemonade Doughnuts

MAKES 12 TO 14 DOUGHNUTS

One summer as I was making lemonade for a weekend barbecue, I decided to shake things up a bit and make a raspberry lemonade. After I made the lemonade, I realized the two flavors would make the most delicious and delightfully pink doughnut. Because who can resist a pink doughnut?

This is a light and fluffy cake doughnut that is baked rather than fried, and then topped with a pink raspberry lemon frosting. The doughnut isn't overly sweet so that the flavor of the frosting can shine, which my kids tell me is amazing.

This is a fun recipe to make with children or if I'm simply craving a pretty pink and tasty doughnut.

For the Raspberry Syrup

6 ounces fresh raspberries

1 tablespoon granulated sugar

1 tablespoon fresh lemon juice

For the Doughnuts

Oil, for greasing

1½ cups all-purpose flour, spoon measured

1 teaspoon baking powder

½ teaspoon salt

½ teaspoon ground nutmeg

½ teaspoon ground ginger

½ cup granulated sugar

1 teaspoon lemon zest

½ cup unsalted butter, softened

1 large egg, room temperature

1 teaspoon vanilla extract

½ cup raspberry jam

½ cup buttermilk

For the Frosting

1½ cups powdered sugar

1 to 2 teaspoons lemon juice

2 tablespoons raspberry syrup

1. To make the raspberry syrup: Place the raspberries, sugar, and lemon juice in a pan and heat over medium heat. Turn the heat to low and simmer for 8 to 10 minutes. Take the pan off the heat and let the puree cool for a few minutes. Then strain all the liquid from the puree. There should be 2 to 3 tablespoons liquid. Reserve the liquid and freeze the puree for smoothies.

2. Preheat the oven to 350°F.

3. Spray two doughnut pans with oil or brush them with oil.

4. Mix together flour, baking powder, salt, nutmeg, and ginger. In the bowl of a stand mixer or another bowl, add the sugar, lemon zest, and softened butter. Mix until well combined and creamy. Add the egg and blend until mixture is light and fluffy.

5. Mix in the vanilla, raspberry jam, and buttermilk. Once it's nicely combined, put some of the batter into a pastry bag with a large tip or into a zip-top bag and cut the tip. Pipe the batter into the doughnut pans.

6. Bake for 10 minutes. Remove from the oven and let cool.

7. To make the frosting, mix together the powdered sugar, lemon juice, and raspberry liquid. Add more powdered sugar or more liquid as necessary. It should be pink and somewhat like a glaze.

8. On one side, dip each doughnut into the glaze and top with your favorite garnish such as sprinkles, mini white chocolate chips, or chopped nuts. Let the glaze set before serving.

Spiced Carrot Cake Cupcakes with Cream Cheese Frosting

MAKES ABOUT 24 CUPCAKES

This is a cake recipe that has been in my family for years. It's the cake my mom always made for special events or occasions. My brother and sister-in-law even had this carrot cake as their wedding cake.

As always, I just can't leave well enough alone. I've adapted this recipe to reflect one of Oregon's largest crops, the hazelnut. I've added hazelnuts instead of walnuts and pumpkin pie spice for additional seasonal flavor, and a few tablespoons of maple syrup are added to the cream cheese frosting.

Lastly, I now make this cake recipe as cupcakes and set them on the dessert table during the holidays. You can dress them up with festive cupcake liners, sweet garnishes, or get artistic with the frosting.

For the Cake

2 cups all-purpose flour

2 teaspoons baking powder

1 teaspoon salt

2½ teaspoons pumpkin pie spice

1½ cups vegetable oil

1¾ cups granulated sugar

4 eggs

2 teaspoons vanilla extract

1 cup chopped hazelnuts (substitute with walnuts if desired), plus more for garnish

2 cups shredded carrots

One 20-ounce can crushed pineapple, completely drained and strained of liquid

1 cup golden raisins

For the Cream Cheese Frosting

½ cup unsalted butter, room temperature

8 ounces cream cheese, room temperature

3 cups powdered sugar

2 tablespoons maple syrup

1. Preheat the oven to 350°F.

2. In a medium bowl, mix together the flour, baking powder, salt, and pumpkin pie spice.

3. In the bowl of a stand mixer or large mixing bowl, mix together the vegetable oil and sugar until nicely combined. Mix in the eggs and vanilla and whisk until creamy.

4. Fold in the hazelnuts, carrots, pineapple, and raisins and stir until combined.

5. Line the muffin pan with cupcake liners and fill each cupcake liner with batter about three-quarters full. Bake for 20 to 25 minutes or until the cupcakes are firm to the touch and golden on top. Let the cupcakes cool completely before frosting.

6. To make the frosting, add the butter and cream cheese to a stand mixer with the whisk attachment. Whisk until smooth.

7. Slowly add the powdered sugar and maple syrup and whisk until smooth and creamy.

8. Add the frosting to a pastry bag and pipe the frosting onto the cooled cupcakes. Garnish with chopped fresh hazelnuts or your desired garnish.

9. Store the cupcakes at room temperature.

Brown Butter and Jam Spoon Cookies

MAKES ABOUT 20 TO 24 COOKIES

I could hang out all day at a dairy farm. There is something so endearing about the sweet faces of dairy cattle, especially when they are happy cows grazing on bright green Oregon grasses. This free-range diet also makes the most delicious butter.

I believe one of my favorite ingredients in both sweet and savory recipes is brown butter. It's nutty in flavor and adds a subtle richness to most any recipe. Luckily, it's the star ingredient in these pretty little Brown Butter and Jam Spoon Cookies.

This is an old Scandinavian recipe (called Lusikkaleivat) given to me by my grandmother. However, we have always called them spoon cookies. Sometimes when I'm in a bit of a hurry, and I don't want to use a spoon to make the cookie, I make this cookie recipe into thumbprint cookies. I use tablespoons of dough, roll them into balls, place them on the cookie sheet, and press my thumb in the center. After they bake, I add a little jelly in the center of the thumbprint.

No matter how I make them, these cookies are a special treat. I typically make them around the holidays, although they are so delicious they often show up year-round in my kitchen.

½ pound (2 sticks) unsalted butter, sliced

½ teaspoon salt

¼ teaspoon nutmeg

2¼ cups all-purpose flour

¾ cup granulated sugar

1 large egg

1 teaspoon vanilla extract

½ cup jam or marmalade

1. Preheat the oven to 350°F. Line a baking sheet with parchment paper.

2. To brown the butter: Heat a heavy-bottomed saucepan over medium heat. Add butter to the pan and let it slowly melt, stirring as needed.

3. Once melted, the butter will begin to get frothy. Begin whisking the butter until the bubbles have evaporated and brown flecks appear. When the butter smells nutty, it has successfully browned.

continued . . .

4. Take the brown butter off the heat and let the butter cool. The butter will go from brown to burnt very quickly, so be sure to watch the butter. If needed, transfer the browned butter to a cool pan.

5. To make the cookies: Mix together the salt, nutmeg, and flour.

6. In a large stand mixer, add cooled brown butter and sugar. Using the paddle attachment, beat until the butter and sugar are thoroughly creamed together, about 5 minutes. It should appear light and fluffy.

7. Add the egg and vanilla and whisk until nicely incorporated. Add the flour mixture to the wet mixture and mix together until the dough is thoroughly combined and pulling away from the sides of the mixing bowl.

8. For a perfect cookie texture, chill the dough in the refrigerator for at least 30 minutes.

9. With an ordinary teaspoon (or tablespoon) you keep in the cutlery drawer, scoop dough into the spoon and press it against the side of the bowl, packing it into the spoon. Smooth the flat side, trimming any excess dough, and then gently slide the spoon-shaped dough out of the spoon and set it flat side down on a parchment paper–lined cookie sheet. Make sure each cookie is uniform because they will be sandwiched together with the jam.

10. Bake the cookies for 12 to 15 minutes, just until they are golden brown, and then take them out of the oven and transfer to a cooling rack.

11. Spread jam on the flat side of one cookie and then sandwich it with another cookie. These cookies will keep for 3 to 5 days, but they never last that long in my house.

Sunflower Seed Butter and Chocolate Chip Cookies

MAKES 20 TO 24 COOKIES

I have a slight obsession with sunflower seed butter. So of course I had to add it to a cookie recipe. Sunflower seed butter is a delicious alternative to peanut butter. It's super creamy and has a slightly toasty flavor that pairs well with chocolate chips. You can often purchase sunflower seed butter wherever peanut butter is sold. Most natural markets stock a nice selection of this tasty treat.

I am a huge fan of Bob's Red Mill products, but I especially enjoy baking with their whole wheat pastry flour, which I've included in this recipe. It adds a lovely depth of flavor and makes the most delicious cookie that is perfectly moist and chewy.

4 tablespoons (½ stick) unsalted butter, room temperature

1 cup dark brown sugar

2 eggs, room temperature

¾ cup sunflower seed butter

1 teaspoon vanilla extract

1½ cups Bob's Red Mill whole wheat pastry flour

1 teaspoon baking soda

Pinch of salt

1½ cups chocolate chips

1. Preheat the oven to 350°F.

2. In a large stand mixer, beat together the butter and brown sugar until it's smooth and creamy, approximately 5 minutes. Add the eggs and continue to mix until once again smooth and creamy.

3. Mix in the sunflower seed butter and vanilla.

4. Mix together flour, baking soda, and salt and then add it to the sun butter mixture and mix until nicely combined. Stir in the chocolate chips.

5. Allow the cookie dough to rest in a cool place for about 10 minutes.

6. Scoop tablespoon-size portions onto a parchment paper–lined cookie sheet. Bake for 10 to 12 minutes. The cookies will be soft in the center but a little crispy on the outside. Let them cool for at least 5 minutes before transferring to a platter or cooling rack.

Hazelnut and Butterscotch Chip Cookies

MAKES 20 TO 24 COOKIES

I have an affinity for butterscotch chips. I adore them so much there is always a package in my pantry just waiting to be used. I probably "tested" this recipe four to five times before I got the perfect cookie. I will admit—it did not make me sad to test this recipe that many times.

The end result is a rich and buttery cookie filled with toasted Oregon hazelnuts and butterscotch chips. They are nutty and slightly chewy and so lovely with morning tea or coffee, or whenever you need a bit of indulgence throughout the day.

2 cups all-purpose flour

1 teaspoon baking soda

½ teaspoon salt

½ pound (2 sticks) unsalted butter, soft

1½ cups packed brown sugar

2 eggs, room temperature

1 teaspoon vanilla extract

1½ cups butterscotch chips

¾ cup chopped hazelnuts

1. Preheat the oven to 350°F.

2. In a medium bowl, whisk together the flour, baking soda, and salt.

3. In the bowl of a stand mixer with the paddle attachment, cream together the butter and brown sugar until light and fluffy, about 5 minutes.

4. Mix in the eggs and vanilla until thoroughly combined. With the mixer on low, slowly add the flour mixture and combine.

5. With a spatula or spoon, stir in the butterscotch chips and chopped hazelnuts. Mix thoroughly. Drop by teaspoonfuls (or use a cookie scoop) onto a parchment paper–lined baking sheet. Place the baking sheet in the oven and bake for 8 to 10 minutes or until the edges of the cookies are golden brown.

6. Remove the baking sheet from the oven and let the cookies cool for 5 minutes before transferring to a cooling rack.

Notes: For extra flavor, toast the hazelnuts in a dry pan over low heat until golden brown before adding them to the cookie dough. Sprinkle a bit of coarse sea salt over the top of the cookies just as they come out of the oven.

DOUBLE J JERSEYS

JON BANSON / MONMOUTH, OREGON

It's evident that Jon and Juli Banson of Double J Jerseys in Monmouth, Oregon, have a passion and deep love for dairy farming. I first met Jon at a special event in Salem sponsored by Organic Valley Co-op. It was at this event that I had the opportunity to speak with Jon in length about how he raises his dairy cattle and how strongly he feels about every detail related to creating quality dairy products. Jon merged with Organic Valley Co-op about 20 years ago, and according to him, it was the best decision he ever made.

He had been considering moving to more organic practices as this type of farming matched what he was already doing. After all, he comes from a family of dairy farmers, and organic farming was the conventional method back when his great-grandfather and grandfather farmed.

Jon says that the conventional world tries to produce bigger and faster. But he feels it's best to work with the natural system and build strong, more sustainable land and soil. He likes to say that he's harvesting sunshine by using the biological process of the soil, the plants, and the cows.

To produce high-quality milk, Jon grows 15 species of plants for the cows to forage. It's a highly mineralized food source due to the healthy soil microbes. The cows rotate large pastures every 34 days to graze on the freshest, best-tasting grass possible; happy cows feeding on high-quality grass will produce the most nutrient-dense milk. Which Jon believes makes the fat profile of his milk much more beneficial to human health.

After visiting the charming Double J Jerseys farm, with its enchanting valley views, and walking the pasture talking to Jon while meeting a group of his beautiful dairy cattle, it's clear that progress and continuing

education are important to him. He's immersed himself in the profession and has become a leader in the industry. Double J Jerseys Farm is committed to providing the freshest, tastiest, and highest-quality milk for their community and beyond.

Vintage Chocolate Spice Cake

SERVES 8 TO 10

I have a few easy dessert recipes that I keep on hand for those impromptu gatherings with family and friends. This is one of those recipes. It's a fluffy and light chocolate cake that reminds me of the sheet cakes my mom used to make. It's not a dark chocolate cake, so I decided to spice it up with cinnamon and cloves and then top it with a decadent chocolate buttercream frosting.

This is a chocolate cake for any occasion, but, because it includes cinnamon and cloves, I especially love to make it during the fall and winter months. It's also a cake made with real butter that I get from Organic Valley and farms such as Double J Jerseys in Monmouth, Oregon. Using a high-quality butter in this recipe truly makes this cake taste delicious and gives it a lovely moist crumb.

For the Cake

Butter and flour for baking dish

6 ounces semisweet chocolate

2 tablespoons hot coffee

8 tablespoons (1 stick) unsalted butter, room temperature

1 cup granulated sugar

2 eggs

1 teaspoon vanilla extract

¾ cup buttermilk

1½ cups all-purpose flour

1 teaspoon baking powder

½ teaspoon baking soda

½ teaspoon salt

1 teaspoon ground cinnamon

½ teaspoon ground cloves

For the Frosting

8 tablespoons (1 stick) unsalted butter, melted

5 tablespoons unsweetened cocoa powder

2 tablespoons warm coffee

2 teaspoons vanilla extract

4 to 6 tablespoons heavy cream

One 16-ounce box powdered sugar

1. Preheat the oven to 350°F. Butter and flour an 8-by-11-inch or 9-by-11-inch baking dish.

2. In a double boiler, melt the chocolate and whisk in the hot coffee. Keep warm.

3. In the bowl of a stand mixer, cream together the butter and sugar until light and fluffy. Mix in one egg at a time and then add the vanilla. Mix in the warm chocolate mixture and, when it's nicely incorporated, mix in buttermilk.

4. In a medium bowl, mix together the flour, baking powder, baking soda, salt, cinnamon, and ground cloves. Add the flour mixture to the wet ingredients and combine.

5. Pour cake batter into the baking dish and bake for 40 to 45 minutes, or until the top of the cake is springy and the center is firm.

6. When the cake is done, remove it from the oven and let it cool completely before adding the frosting.

7. To make the frosting, add melted butter, cocoa powder, warm coffee, vanilla, and heavy cream to the bowl of a stand mixer. Blend together until nicely combined. Then add the powdered sugar and mix until thoroughly combined. It will be light and fluffy.

8. Frost the cake and serve. I usually have a little frosting left over. I love to spread frosting between graham crackers as a little afternoon treat with tea.

Sweet Potato Coconut Tarts with Scotch-Laced Caramel Sauce

MAKES 10 TO 12 4-INCH TARTS

This recipe has quite the story. It was originally my mom's pumpkin pie recipe that I made into little pumpkin tarts. At some point, I decided to skip the sweetened condensed milk, add a little sugar, and substitute with coconut milk. It turned out to be a delicious alternative. But it still wasn't perfect. Instead of pumpkin, I decided to use sweet potato puree, which I adore. To finish, I added a Scotch-laced caramel sauce. And there you have it. My Sweet Potato Coconut Tarts with Scotch-Laced Caramel Sauce were born.

You might be wondering why Scotch and not bourbon or even brandy. Simply because I adore good Scotch. My caramel sauce had to include it. But feel free to spike your caramel sauce with whatever you may have on hand or omit the libations if you'd like.

In a pinch or to save time, I skip preparing the pâte brisée and purchase ready-made pie dough. This works just as well.

For the Pie Dough (Pâte Brisée)

1¼ cups pastry flour

1 teaspoon granulated sugar

½ teaspoon salt

6 tablespoons (¾ stick) cold unsalted butter, cut into ½-inch pieces

1 large egg

1 teaspoon ice water

For the Sweet Potato Coconut Filling

One 15-ounce can organic sweet potato puree (you can also substitute pumpkin puree)

½ cup granulated sugar

1 cup organic canned coconut milk (do not use "lite" coconut milk)

1 teaspoon vanilla extract

1½ teaspoons ground cinnamon

¼ teaspoon fresh grated nutmeg

Pinch of salt

3 large eggs

For the Scotch Caramel Sauce

1 cup granulated sugar

6 tablespoons (¾ stick) unsalted butter

½ cup heavy cream

Pinch of salt

1 to 2 tablespoons Scotch (or whiskey or bourbon, if you prefer)

Whipped cream, to serve

1. Make the pâte brisée: If you don't have pastry flour on hand, combine two parts all-purpose flour with one part cake flour. (I keep this combination handy in a separate container, so I always have some ready to use.)

2. Combine the flour, sugar, and salt in the bowl of a food processor. Pulse a few times to mix.

3. Add the cold butter to the flour mixture and pulse a few more times until the butter and flour resemble coarse pea-size pieces or a coarse meal.

4. As you pulse the food processor, add the egg and water and pulse only until the dough is holding together in one piece.

5. Turn out the dough onto a floured surface and knead just a few times. Then form the dough into a disc. Wrap in plastic wrap and refrigerate for an hour or so, or overnight. Often, I'll make several batches of pâte brisée and then keep them wrapped in the freezer, pulling them out when I know I'll need them.

6. Remove the chilled disc from the refrigerator and roll it out with a wooden rolling pin to about 1/8 to 1/4 inch thick. With a biscuit cutter or mouth of a drinking glass, cut out discs large enough to press into mini tart pans. Fill all the mini tart pans with the pie crust and then place in the refrigerator until you are ready to fill them with the sweet potato filling.

7. Make the Sweet Potato Coconut Filling: In a stand mixer, combine all the ingredients until well blended.

8. Preheat the oven to 350°F. Place all the prepped mini tart pans on a baking sheet and fill each mini tart pan with sweet potato coconut filling.

9. Place the baking sheet of tarts in the oven and bake for 35 to 40 minutes or until the filling is nicely firm and the crusts are golden.

10. While the tarts are baking, prepare the caramel sauce. In a medium saucepan over medium-low heat, mix together the sugar, butter, heavy cream, and a pinch of salt.

11. Whisk the ingredients until it comes to a boil and then let it simmer for 5 to 8 minutes or until it thickens. Lastly, stir in the Scotch. Keep slightly warm.

12. Once the tarts are done, remove them from the oven and let them cool. Place each tart on a small dessert plate. Drizzle with a little caramel sauce and then top with whipped cream. Toasted coconut also makes a delicious garnish.

WOODEN SHOE TULIP FARM

WOODBURN, OREGON

Oregonians are fortunate to have a plethora of flower farms in the state. One of the largest flower farms is the Wooden Shoe Tulip Farm, which is located in the middle of the Willamette Valley in Woodburn, Oregon.

It was an early, cool April morning when I visited the Wooden Shoe Tulip Farm. As I was driving up the winding country road under an overcast sky, I could see specks of pinks and purples floating on the horizon. As I drove closer, the sea of color bloomed into the most beautiful ocean of tulips.

Wooden Shoe Tulip Farm owes its origins to the marriage of Ross and Dorothy Iverson in 1950. The Iverson family began growing tulips in 1974, and by the early 1980s, they started the Wooden Shoe Bulb Company. Many years later it became the Wooden Shoe Tulip Farm. The farm now grows about 80 different varieties of tulips along with other farm crops throughout the year.

In 1985, Wooden Shoe Tulip Farm began opening their farm to the public. It was such a huge success they now open their fields from the end of March through the first week of May every year. According to a Wooden Shoe family member, "The Iverson family looks forward to the tulip festival each year. They feel it's a place that brings families together to make lasting memories for years to come."

Although the tulip season spans a little over a month, Wooden Shoe Tulip Farm also hosts a variety of special events throughout the year, from farm dinners to wine tastings at the Wooden Shoe Vineyards to barbecues and fun runs that benefit local charities.

Cardamom-Spiced Hot Chocolate

SERVES 2

I believe this sipping chocolate has to be one of my favorite indulgences. It's certainly what popped into my mind while roaming the tulip fields at the Wooden Shoe Tulip Farm one cold spring morning. It's one of those beverages that feels like a soft, cozy blanket that wraps you in its warmth with every sip. It's an indulgence, and especially comforting on a cool morning or as an afternoon treat during the winter months.

For the best flavor, purchase fresh cardamom pods. They last about 6 months and I use them in other dessert recipes or sauces, curries, soups, and stews.

2 cups whole milk

2 green cardamom pods, crushed so the seeds are exposed (I crush them with a mortar and pestle)

4 ounces of your favorite chocolate, chopped

2 tablespoons granulated sugar or your choice of sweetener (if using bittersweet chocolate)

Whipped cream and chocolate shavings, for garnish

1. In a small saucepan, heat the milk over low heat. As it begins to warm, add the cardamom pods, chocolate, and sugar. Stirring, bring the milk just to a simmer, about 180°F. You don't want it to boil. Once tiny bubbles form around the edges of the pan and the chocolate is melted, remove it from the heat and let it sit for a minute or two covered.

2. Strain the hot chocolate into two mugs and top with fresh whipped cream or chocolate shavings. Serve immediately.

Note: I like to use a true "sipping chocolate" for this recipe. You can find it in the hot cocoa or baking areas of your market.

DRESSINGS, CONDIMENTS, SALSAS, AND SAUCES

Easy Dinner Salad Vinaigrette

MAKES 1¼ CUPS

This is what I call my house dressing. It's the dressing that I make every week and keep in a jelly jar in my refrigerator. During different seasons, I adjust ingredients a bit, using honey instead of maple syrup and white wine vinegar instead of apple cider vinegar.

It's perfect for last-minute salads, roasted or grilled vegetables, as a marinade for chicken or shrimp, or a quick sauce for salmon. I also use this dressing on the Shaved Brussels Sprouts Salad with Winter Squash, Dried Cherries, and Bacon with Maple Vinaigrette on page 91.

¼ cup apple cider vinegar

¾ cup high-quality extra virgin olive oil

¼ cup maple syrup

1 tablespoon Dijon mustard

1 tablespoon stone-ground mustard

2 teaspoons yellow mustard

1 large clove garlic, minced

1 teaspoon chopped fresh thyme leaves

1 tablespoon lemon juice

Splash of water

Salt and pepper, to taste

1. Place all the ingredients in a 12- to 16-ounce jar with a lid. Shake until all the ingredients are well combined. Or add ingredients to a blender and blend until combined.

2. Refrigerate for up to 1 week.

Kristin's Sweet and Spicy Blue Cheese Dressing

MAKES 1¼ CUPS

My twin sister (and fellow chef) gave me this lovely recipe almost 20 years ago. I still make it today and it remains one of my favorite dressing recipes. This is the salad dressing recipe to use your favorite and most delicious blue cheese in, such as Rogue Creamery blue cheese. During the summer months, I use the dressing over grilled romaine lettuce. During the winter, it's divine over iceberg or butter lettuce. This is also lovely when paired with the Oregon Shrimp Salad with Spicy Seafood Dressing on page 101.

¾ cup extra virgin olive oil

3 tablespoons champagne vinegar

1 clove garlic, minced

1 tablespoon finely minced shallot

1 tablespoon yellow mustard

1 tablespoon ketchup

1 tablespoon granulated sugar

2 tablespoons water

2 ounces Rogue Creamery blue cheese

Salt and pepper, to taste

1. Whisk together the olive oil, vinegar, garlic, shallot, mustard, ketchup, sugar, and water until thoroughly combined. Stir in the cheese, season to taste with salt and pepper, and serve over your favorite salad greens.

2. Refrigerate for up to 1 week.

Easy Herb Vinaigrette

MAKES ABOUT ⅔ CUP

Backyard gardens and urban gardens, such as Oasis of Change in Portland, grow a plethora of fresh vegetables and herbs. It seems parsley will grow almost year-round in my garden given the right temperatures. And I've been known to keep a chive plant thriving for almost an entire year, which makes midwinter a little more delicious.

I love pairing parsley or Italian parsley with chives in this lovely little vinaigrette. It's delightful on winter citrus salads with avocado and ancient grain salad bowls, and it's lovely over fish. I also toss it with Lemon-Herb Roasted New Potatoes on page 107 or drizzle it over my Oregon Shrimp Salad with Spicy Seafood Dressing on page 101.

½ cup extra virgin olive oil

2 tablespoons apple cider vinegar

2 tablespoons honey

2 tablespoons chopped fresh Italian parsley

1 tablespoon chopped fresh chives

Salt and pepper, to taste

1. Place all the ingredients in a jar with a lid and shake until smooth and combined. Season to taste with salt and pepper.

2. Refrigerate for up to 1 week.

Lemon Vinaigrette

MAKES ABOUT ⅔ CUP

I believe every home cook should have an easy lemon vinaigrette recipe. This is the workhorse of vinaigrettes and it's truly delicious on most salads and vegetables. For an "in a pinch" meal, I use it over a quick pan-cooked fish. I also toss it with my Lemon-Herb Roasted New Potatoes on page 107 or Roasted Green Bean Salad with Dried Cherries, Toasted Pine Nuts, and Goat Cheese on page 114.

½ cup extra virgin olive oil

Zest of 1 lemon

3 tablespoons lemon juice

1 shallot, minced (or see additional method below)

1 teaspoon spicy brown mustard

1 teaspoon granulated sugar

Salt and pepper, to taste

1. First method: Add the olive oil, lemon zest, lemon juice, shallot, mustard, and sugar to a jelly jar. Place the lid on top and shake until thoroughly combined. Season to taste with salt and pepper. You can whisk the ingredients as well.

2. Second method: I double the recipe, add everything to my small food processor or blender, and puree. Season to taste with salt and pepper. This gives me a well-blended vinaigrette and then I don't have to mince the shallot.

3. Refrigerate for up to 1 week.

OASIS OF CHANGE

DOV JUDD AND KATHRYN CANNON / PORTLAND, OREGON

Kathryn Cannon and Dov Judd have truly found an Oasis of Change for their Portland community. I first heard about this cutting-edge urban farm and wellness center when I met both Kathryn and Dov at a Portland Culinary Alliance gathering. They shared with me the concept for Oasis of Change and I was immediately intrigued.

Dov, a pediatric play therapist, and Kathryn, a peer-to-peer support specialist, left their respective jobs to seek new ways in which to use their talents. Dov says, "We dreamed of a place that celebrates life and integrates all aspects of health."

On a gorgeous summer day, I visited Oasis of Change and followed Dov around the property that houses a 10,000-square-foot retreat center, a beautiful Victorian house built in 1893, and the flourishing urban farm that is the center of it all. Oasis of Change is located in the city and sits on a busy neighborhood street, but once I walked onto the property, it seemed like the most peaceful place to be.

This serene urban farm and wellness center is a new concept in community wellness, prevention, and intervention. Oasis of Change hosts cooking classes, community events, on-site holis-

tic and naturopathic medical practitioners, yoga classes, pop-up farm-to-table dinners, and special evening concerts. It is food-focused and wellness-driven, and provides accessible food-based experiences to inspire good health, happiness, and community around food.

Dov and Kathryn believe that taking a positive, open-minded approach to cooking and food choices is the best way to get people excited about good food and vibrant health.

BASICS MARKET

PORTLAND, OREGON

There is a new market in town, and it's changing the way we shop for food. Basics Market is a market, a classroom, and a gathering place, nourishing the community from the ground up. It's a collective of farmers, entrepreneurs, culinary experts, nutritionists, and natural foods veterans inspired to nurture health through food.

The market is small and accessible and focused on just what we need to cook a healthful delicious meal at home. They partner with local sustainable producers whenever they can and work together to keep prices accessible. They are also working to make good food more accessible by eliminating the traditional layers of distribution and going direct from farm to store as much as possible.

As customers walk through the market they will notice several Basics Meal Stations throughout the store. These are stations that make it easy to find all the ingredients for a chef-inspired recipe. Just choose the recipe you want to cook, and all the ingredients will be located at one meal station.

In addition to the meal stations, you'll find a protein counter with locally sourced meats and seafood; local, organic cheese and dairy selections; fresh, seasonal produce; pantry staples; frozen foods; grab-and-go items; and wine and beer. The market also has a classroom for nutrition classes, interactive cooking demos, and kitchen skills classes taught by Basics' culinary and nutrition mentors.

They are also giving back to the local community by setting up a Basics Mini Market and Food Pantry located within Faubion Elementary and Concordia University to provide students and staff access to nutritious foods right within school walls. It's part of an integrated effort to ensure that every child can fulfill their potential.

These are truly markets driven by purpose—to support good health and strong communities. This is an Oregon company that supports local farmers, local food producers, and local communities one Basics Market at a time.

Avocado Dressing and Sauce

MAKES ABOUT 1½ CUPS

This is my answer to bringing home too many avocados that all ripen at the same time. Like many, I make my fair share of avocado toast, but avocados also make the most luscious dressing. I use this dressing on salads such as the Layered Cornbread Salad (page 96), veggie and salmon bowls, grilled shrimp, and basically anything that might pair well with avocados.

If I'm using this as a sauce for salmon or veggie tacos, I substitute the lemon and parsley with lime zest, lime juice, and cilantro.

1 medium ripe avocado

Zest of 1 lemon

2 tablespoons lemon juice

1 clove garlic

1 medium shallot

2 tablespoons extra virgin olive oil

2 tablespoons chopped fresh parsley or cilantro

¼ cup water, or as needed for desired consistency

1. Add all of the ingredients to a blender and puree until smooth. Add additional water for desired consistency. Season to taste with salt and pepper.

2. This dressing is best used the day it's made, but you can refrigerate for up to 24 hours.

Quick Pickled Red Onions

MAKES ABOUT 1 CUP

When I'm in Portland, before heading back home, I love to stop by Basics Market for a few items to make dinner. I can always find fresh ingredients and pantry staples to prepare a meal or make these delicious Quick Pickled Onions.

I love them tossed on salads, vegetables, and tacos, or over an afternoon snack of salmon lox and goat cheese on crackers. They're also beautiful served on antipasti platters or cheese plates, served with my Grilled Salmon Tacos with Pineapple Cilantro Slaw and Chipotle Lime Sauce (page 140) or included in the Mexican Corn and Tomato Salad (page 97).

½ cup water

½ cup rice wine vinegar

1 tablespoon granulated sugar

1 teaspoon salt

5 to 8 whole peppercorns

1 large red onion, thinly sliced

1. Whisk together the water, vinegar, sugar, salt, and peppercorns.

2. Pack sliced red onion into a lidded jar and then pour the pickling mixture over the onions. Let them sit at room temperature for about an hour.

3. Cover and refrigerate for up to 1 week.

Summer Spanish-Style Salsa Verde

MAKES 1 CUP

I make this quick summer salsa verde to garnish grilled fish, shrimp, or chicken. It's also delicious sprinkled over grilled vegetables. After grabbing beautiful summer tomatoes from Bear Branch Farms, I slathered them in this salsa verde and topped them with toasted pine nuts. It adds a burst of color with loads of fresh herbal and citrus flavors.

½ cup Italian parsley

6 to 8 fresh mint leaves

1 clove garlic

2 anchovies

1 tablespoon capers

Squeeze of lemon

⅓ cup good quality extra virgin olive oil

Salt and pepper, to taste

1. Add the parsley, mint, garlic, anchovies, capers, lemon juice, and olive oil to a food processor or blender. Pulse until you have a nice rough-chopped salsa consistency. You can also hand-chop the ingredients for more texture.

2. Season to taste with salt and pepper.

3. Store in a glass jar in the refrigerator for up to 24 hours.

Cucumber Jalapeño Salsa

MAKES 2 CUPS

A few summers ago, I planted zucchini and cucumber in my garden. However, the plants I thought were zucchini were actually cucumber. By mid-July I had an explosion of cucumbers. I couldn't give them away or eat them fast enough. So I started making this salsa recipe that was inspired by one of my favorite restaurants on the Oregon coast, Local Ocean Seafood.

This salsa is delicious on tacos, ceviche, and grilled seafood; over sliced avocados; or with tortilla chips.

½ red onion, diced

2 medium cucumbers, peeled, seeded, and diced

2 medium to large jalapeños, seeded and diced

½ cup chopped fresh cilantro

1 tablespoon chopped fresh parsley

1 teaspoon chopped fresh mint

Juice of 1 lime

½ teaspoon granulated sugar

1 tablespoon extra virgin olive oil

Salt and pepper, to taste

1. Place the onion, cucumbers, jalapeños, cilantro, parsley, mint, lime juice, sugar, and olive oil in a bowl and toss to combine. Season to taste with salt and pepper. Use immediately.

Note: As the salsa sits for a while, it will weep. Drain any excess liquid that forms.

BEAR BRANCH FARMS

JANIS AND NATE NEWSOM / STAYTON, OREGON

Janis and Nate always loved gardening, so, when that love of gardening grew into multiple large gardens at their home in California, they decided it was time to buy a farm where they could put their love of growing food to good use.

With eight children in tow at the time, they sold everything and put their life savings into what is now known as Bear Branch Farms in Stayton, Oregon. Bear Branch Farms is in its fifth season and they are continually excited about offering healthy, local, pesticide-free food to their community.

They use high-quality heirloom, artisan, and organic seed practices, with biodiversity, intensive soil testing, and care being their focus. They use a gentle till design to help keep their soil fertile without hauling topsoil. Their nutrient-dense produce is CNG (Certified Naturally Grown).

Janis and Nate are advocates of organically grown standards and are on a mission to provide healthy, safe, local foods beyond what is required by certification. They believe that "if our kids can't run through the fields and eat it unwashed, neither should you!"

It's clear that Janis and Nate, and their children, love what they do. This family farm is brimming with smiles and jovial conversation, beautiful produce, and flowers. They have a farm pick-up garden that adds extra produce to the full share CSAs (community supported agriculture). And Bear Branch Farms offers a "farm stay" at their stunning, large farmhouse that overlooks the vegetable fields. They also offer a "rustic cabin stay" and a "tiny house stay" for a cozy farm setting.

At the end of my visit, Janis and Nate generously sent me off with a large bag of jalapeños, sweet onions, and fresh and bright red hothouse tomatoes—the best tasting tomatoes I had all summer! Find out more about Bear Branch Farms on their website, Instagram, and Facebook page.

KIRSCH FAMILY FARMS, INC.

BRENDA AND MATT FRKETICH / ST. PAUL, OREGON

When Brenda Frketich was growing up on the beautiful Kirsch Family Farms in St. Paul, Oregon, she never dreamed she'd take it over. But that's exactly what happened. She attended Loyola Marymount University and earned a degree in business management. She had planned to go to law school following graduation, but during her second year of college, she stayed in Los Angeles to work over the summer. It was the very first harvest she had ever missed.

Brenda said this was a turning point in her life. She realized how much she loved not just the farm, but agriculture, the community, and the industry in general. In 2006, after graduation, Brenda returned home and worked a two-year internship on the farm, just to be certain farming was the career she wanted.

Today, Brenda and her husband, Matt Frketich, own Kirsch Family Farms, which grows two of Oregon's largest crops: grass seed and hazelnuts. They also grow vegetable seeds, vegetables, wheat, and clover.

Brenda has become an advocate for the farming community and a voice for Oregon farms. She's an active member of the agriculture industry and is currently on the board of several agricultural organizations. Brenda says, "I feel honored that I get to work within a culture such as agriculture that embraces the past, present, and future with a deep respect for all three."

As a third-generation farmer now raising the fourth generation, she couldn't be prouder of her family's history of integrity and hard work. She's happy to say that, while she and her family are still using tools her grandpa used, they are also part of an industry that is on the cutting edge of technology and innovation. Being a part of this industry has always made Brenda proud of what they do at Kirsch Family Farms.

Spiced Yogurt Sauce

MAKES 2 CUPS

When my youngest daughter was little, she lived on yogurt and apple sauce. I'm not sure how her affinity for these two things started, but they were a staple in her lunch box. To entice her to eat grilled or roasted vegetables, I served this spiced yogurt sauce on the side. She happily doused her grilled eggplant with yogurt sauce and declared it completely delicious.

Today, my entire family adores this Spiced Yogurt Sauce served with roasted or grilled vegetables, falafel, or chicken. Sometimes I serve the Chermoula-Marinated Grilled Vegetable and Pineapple Skewers on page 116 with this sauce rather than the Chermoula.

1 tablespoon extra virgin olive oil

½ cup finely diced sweet onions

1 clove garlic, minced

2 cups plain whole-milk yogurt

1 teaspoon garam masala

1 teaspoon grated fresh ginger

1. In a small pan, heat the olive oil over medium heat and cook the onions. When the onions are soft and wilted, add the garlic and cook 1 minute longer. Take the pan off the heat.

2. In a medium bowl, mix together the yogurt, garam masala, and fresh ginger. Stir in the onions and garlic.

3. This sauce is best used immediately but it can be kept covered in the refrigerator for up to 24 hours.

Spiced Chocolate Sauce

MAKES 1 CUP

This is a special chocolate sauce I use when I need dessert in a pinch. I usually serve the sauce with a prepared chocolate pound cake or homemade brownies and then top it with sliced fresh papaya. This sauce can also be used over the Vintage Chocolate Spice Cake (page 184) instead of the buttercream frosting.

The sauce is tasty over ice cream, fresh berries, and bananas, or when stirred into warm milk.

8 ounces dark chocolate, crumbled

½ cup heavy cream

½ cup water

1 teaspoon cinnamon

6 drops coffee extract or almond extract

Pinch cayenne pepper (optional)

1. In a double boiler over medium-low heat, add the dark chocolate and melt it until it's smooth. Take it off the heat.

2. In a small saucepan over medium-low heat, add the heavy cream and water. When the liquid is hot, whisk in the melted chocolate and cinnamon. Take the sauce off the heat and whisk in the extract and a pinch of cayenne pepper if desired.

3. The sauce can be refrigerated up to 1 week.

Hazelnut Romesco Sauce

MAKES ABOUT 1½ CUPS

Hazelnut trees are simply beautiful. I had the chance to meander through an orchard at Kirsch Family Farms with Brenda and Matt Frketich. The orchards are quite dreamy in appearance and when I walk deep into an orchard, it almost feels otherworldly.

During my visit at Kirsch Family Farms, I was able to get the scoop on these popular Oregon nuts that are actually the official state nut. Oregon produces 99 percent of the nation's crop of filberts, which are known in the market as hazelnuts. The nuts mature during the summer months, turning from green to shades of hazel nestled in a husk, and then harvested in late September or October after they've fallen to the ground.

As you can imagine, we use a lot of hazelnuts in my house. I roast them for snacking, use them in baked goods, for crusting fish or chicken, and in this bright orange-red romesco sauce. I love to pair this sauce with roast pork or chicken and sometimes I serve it with warm, crusty bread just for dipping.

2 medium to large red bell peppers, roasted, peeled, and seeded

1 large ripe tomato

3 cloves garlic

1 tablespoon chopped fresh parsley

½ cup chopped, toasted hazelnuts

1 tablespoon smoked paprika

2 tablespoons sherry vinegar

Salt and pepper, to taste

1. Place all the ingredients in a blender or food processor and puree until smooth. Season to taste with salt and pepper.

2. This sauce can be served immediately or kept covered in the refrigerator for up to 3 days.

Quick Five Spice Nectarine Chutney

ABOUT 1½ CUPS

Fruit and fish is one of my favorite ingredient combinations, which is how this quick nectarine chutney happened. Summers in Oregon produce a bevy of stone fruit. Nectarines, especially white nectarines, are sweet and juicy and pair well with savory ingredients. I've added a little five spice powder to the chutney, which creates a flavorful and fragrant sauce.

I like to pair this chutney with roasted or grilled meat, poultry, and, of course, fish.

2 tablespoons unsalted butter

½ cup diced onions

½ cup diced red peppers

1 clove garlic, minced

2 pounds fresh nectarines, peeled, pitted, and chopped (3 to 4 cups)

⅓ cup golden raisins

¼ cup brown sugar

1 teaspoon five spice powder (see note below to make your own five spice powder)

Pinch crushed red pepper flakes

2 tablespoons apple cider vinegar

Salt and pepper, to taste

1. Add the butter to a large saucepan over medium heat. Add onions and red peppers and cook until soft and caramelized. Stir in the garlic and cook 1 minute longer.

2. Stir in the nectarines, raisins, brown sugar, five spice powder, red pepper flakes, and apple cider vinegar. Bring the ingredients to a boil and then reduce heat to a simmer. Cook until the fruit is reduced and thickened, 10 to 15 minutes.

3. Take the pan off the heat and season to taste with salt and pepper.

4. Refrigerate for up to 1 week.

Note: To make five spice powder, mix together 3 tablespoons cinnamon, 5 star anise, 1½ teaspoons fennel seeds, 1½ teaspoons black peppercorns, and ½ teaspoon ground cloves. Combine in a spice blender or spice mill and blend until finely ground. Keep in an airtight container for up to 3 months. Makes about ¼ cup.

ACKNOWLEDGMENTS

My sincerest thanks to my agent Jessica Alvarez, for your support, encouragement, and committed belief in me and my work. To my talented editor, Isabel McCarthy; Editorial Director Ann Treistman; copy editor Natalie Eilbert; and the brilliant team at The Countryman Press, thank you for making my work shine.

Thanks and gratitude to all the farmers, ranchers, and food and drink producers I had the opportunity to meet and to write about. Your gracious hospitality and passion for your work is inspiring. Many thanks to Victoria Binning at the Oregon State University Extension Program for your advice and valuable information.

Huge thanks to my incredible team of recipe testers: Tiffany Aske, Jessica Harper, Dwana Lashover, Sheri Ogilvie, Tawnya Penny, Eileen Smith, Marni Zarr, fellow food writer Kelley McKone Epstien, fellow food writer Samantha Ferraro, and finally, my friend Judy Niver, for all your dedicated support and the second set of eyes. Thank you to my friend and professional editor, Maresa Giovannini, for your valuable feedback and brilliant advice.

My heartfelt thanks to one of my dearest friends, Kristen Allen-Bentsen, who not only tested recipes for this book but has been my cheerleader and fierce supporter for almost two decades. Thanks to my friend and fellow author, Chef Laurie Pfalzer, for your rad pastry skills and brilliant culinary advice. Thank you to Food Innovation Chef Sarah House, for your spot-on recipe advice and recommendations.

Many thanks to the very talented Max Husbands, taste tester extraordinaire, for always giving me the best recipe ideas while sampling my food. Thank you to my friend and fellow author, Lori Rice, for your sage advice and photography savvy, and to my friend, fellow chef, and author, Maya Wilson, for your cherished friendship, inspiration, and advice.

To my loving siblings, Kristin Bryan and Cameron Taylor, your devotion to our life's journey together has been the light in my darkness and the peace in my heart. I am so grateful for your ardent support, thoughtful words of wisdom, and unconditional love.

My heartfelt love and thanks to my family: Paula Galofre Taylor, Kevin Bryan, Sharon and Alan Taylor, Aubrey Taylor Wade, Carolina Taylor, Taylor Bryan Tomalski, Brianna Bryan, Sebastian Taylor, Max Bryan, and Ellen and Don Taylor, for your unwavering love and support throughout this project. I love you all!

To my remarkable and loving daughters, Alexandria and Amelia Bennett, you are my heart, my constant inspiration, and you will forever make my life complete. I couldn't be more proud to be your mom.

Finally, my deepest, heartfelt thanks to my amazing husband, Craig Bennett. You are my forever partner in this food-, farm-, and travel-loving life. Thank you for your unwavering encouragement to jump into everything with love and passion, to keep growing, to keep dreaming, and to keep following my heart because that's what life is all about. I love you.

PHOTO CREDITS

All photos taken by Karista Bennett unless specified below.

Page 10: Betty Boyce

Page 16: Juniper and the Sea Photography

Page 26: Shawn Linehan

Page 32: Bermudez Family Farm

Page 41: Bites Restaurant

Page 48: Youngberg Hill Wine Country Inn and Vineyard

Page 51 and 53 (top right): Maylin Chavez

Page 71: Trav Williams, Broken Banjo Photography

Page 75: Local Ocean Seafood

Page 80 (top right): Newport Fishermen's Wives

Page 87 (top right): Cowhorn Vineyard & Garden

Pages 98–100: Ty Mead

Page 106: The Croft Farm

Page 110: Maya Dooley

Page 122: Cool Notion Photography

Page 124–26: Andrea Johnson

Page 130: SakéOne

Page 132: Port Orford Sustainable Seafood

Page 135: Chad Brown

Page 173 (top and bottom): Rebekah Jule Photography

Page 174: Bob's Red Mill

Page 183: Organic Valley Farms

Page 196: Basics Market, Mary Paganelli

Page 199: Bear Branch Farms

Page 200: Kirsch Family Farms

PEOPLE AND PLACES

Abbey Creek Vineyard
Bertony Faustin, Farmer/Owner
Page 135
North Plains, Oregon
www.abbeycreekvineyard.com
www.instagram.com/abbeycreekwine

Basics Market
Chuck Eggert, Founder
Page 196
Portland, Oregon
www.basicsmarket.com
www.instagram.com/basicsmarket

Bear Branch Farms
Janis and Nate Newsom, Farmers/Owners
Page 199
Stayton, Oregon
www.bearbranchfarms.com
www.instagram.com/bearbranchfarms

Bermudez Family Farm
Malinda Bermudez, Farmer/Owner
Page 32
Dallas, Oregon
bermudezfamilyfarm.blogspot.com
www.facebook.com/bermudezfamilyfarm
bermudezfamilyfarm.blogspot.com

Bites Restaurant
Fon and Thomas Gilstrap, Owners
Page 41
www.bitesrestaurant.com
www.instagram.com/bitesrestaurant

Bob's Red Mill Natural Foods
Bob Moore, Founder
Page 174
Milwaukee, Oregon
www.bobsredmill.com
www.instagram.com/bobsredmill/

Cody Wood, Farmer
Page 154
Junction City, Oregon
www.cattailcreeklamb.com
www.instagram.com/codywould/

Cória Estates
Aurora Cória, Winemaker
Luis and Janis Cória, Farmer/Owners
Page 100
Salem, Oregon
www.coriaestates.com
www.instagram.com/coriaestates

Cowhorn Vineyard & Garden
Bill and Barbara Steele, Farmers/Owners/Winemakers
Page 87
Jacksonville, Oregon
www.cowhornwine.com
www.instagram.com/cowhornwines

The Croft Farm
Vail & Greg, Farmers
Page 106
Sauvie Island, Oregon
www.thecroftfarm.com
www.instagram.com/thecroftfarm

Double J Jerseys
Jon Bansen, Dairy Farmer
Page 183
Monmouth, Oregon
www.organicvalley.coop/our-farmers/10197/

Fiddlehead Farm
Katie Coppoletta and Tayne Reeve, Farmers
Page 26
Corbett, Oregon
www.fiddleheadfarmers.com
www.instagram.com/fiddleheadfarmer

Fisher Ridge Farm
Sue and Ralph Fisher, Farmers
Page 160
Sublimity, Oregon
www.facebook.com/fisherridgefarm

Hoffman Farms Store
Jay and Kelly Hoffman, Farmers
Page 173
Scholls, Oregon
www.hoffmanfarmsstore.com
www.instagram.com/hoffmanfarmsstore

Hood River Lavender Farms
Page 168
Odell, Oregon
www.hoodriverlavender.com
www.instagram.com/hoodriverlavender

Kirsch Family Farms
Brenda and Matt Frketich, Farmers/Owners
Page 200
St. Paul, Oregon
www.nuttygrass.com

Local Ocean Seafood
Chef Enrique Sanchez, Executive Chef
Page 75
Newport, Oregon
www.localocean.net
www.instagram.com/localoceanseafoods

Lucky Crow Farm
Eden Olsen, Owner/Farmer
Page 92
Monmouth, Oregon
www.luckycrowfarm.com
www.instagram.com/luckycrowfarm

Marion Polk Food Share Youth Farm
Jared Hibbard-Swanson, Farm Manager
Page 112
Salem, Oregon
www.marionpolkfoodshare.org/programs/youth-farm

Martson Farm
Rick Martson, Farmer/Owner
Page 84
Molalla, Oregon
www.martsonfarm.com
www.instagram.com/martson.farm

Moon River Farm
Kayleigh Hillert and Lily Strauss, Farmers/Owners
Page 110
Nehalem, Oregon
www.moonriverfarmers.com
www.instagram.com/moonriverfarmers

The Mushroomery
Jennifer Macone and Dustin Olsen, Farmers/Owners
Page 64
Lebanon, Oregon
www.themushroomery.net
www.facebook.com/The-Mushroomery

Nehalem River Ranch
Jared Gardner, Farmer/Owner
Page 71
Nehalem, Oregon
www.nehalemriverranch.com
www.instagram.com/nehalem_river_ranch

Newport Fishermen's Wives
Page 80
Newport, Oregon
www.newportfishermenswives.com
www.facebook.com/NewportFishermensWives

Oasis of Change
Dov Judd and Kathryn Cannon, Farmers/Owners
Page 195
Portland, Oregon
www.oasisofchange.com
www.instagram.com/oasisofchange

Olympia Oyster Bar
Chef Maylin Chavez, Owner
Page 53
Portland, Oregon
www.instagram.com/olympiaoysterbar

Pitchfork and Crow Farms
Carri Heisler and Jeff Bramlett, Farmers/Owners
Page 30
Lebanon, Oregon
www.pitchforkandcrow.com
www.instagram.com/pitchforkandcrow

Port Orford Sustainable Seafood
Aaron Longton, Chris Aiello, and Darrell Cobb, Founders
Page 132
Port Orford, Oregon
www.posustainableseafood.com
www.instagram.com/portorfordsustainableseafood

Rafns' Restaurant
Chef Nathan Rafn and Rochelle Rafn, Owners
Page 122
Salem, Oregon
www.rafns.com
www.instagram.com/rafnslocalfoods

Red Bird Acres
Laura and Robin Sage, Farmers/Owners
Page 144
Corvallis, Oregon
www.redbirdacresfarm.com
www.instagram.com/redbirdacres

Rogue Ales
Page 149
Newport, Oregon
www.rogue.com
www.instagram.com/rogueales

Rogue Creamery and Dairy
Page 164
Central Point, Oregon
www.roguecreamery.com
www.instagram.com/roguecreamery

SakéOne Brewery
Page 130
Forest Grove, Oregon
www.sakeone.com
www.instagram.com/sakeoneoregon

Sweet Delilah Flower Farm
Chelsea Willis, Farmer/Owner
Page 210
Sauvie Island, Oregon
www.sweetdelilahfarm.com
www.instagram.com/sweetdelilahfarm

Unger Farms
Kathy and Matt Unger, Farmers/Owners
Page 55
Cornelius, Oregon
www.ungerfarms.com
www.instagram.com/ungerfarms

Willamette Valley Vineyards
Jim Bernau, Owner/Winemaker
Page 126
Turner, Oregon
www.wvv.com
www.instagram.com/willamettevalleyvineyards

Witte Flower Farm
Kristin LaMont and Mike Witte, Farmers/Owners
Page 19
Salem, Oregon
www.witteflowerfarm.com
www.instagram.com/wittefarm

Wooden Shoe Tulip Farm
Page 190
Woodburn, Oregon
www.woodenshoe.com
www.instagram.com/woodenshoefarm

Youngberg Hill
Wayne Bailey, Owner/Winemaker
Page 48
McMinnville, Oregon
www.youngberghill.com
www.instagram.com/youngberg_hill

INDEX

Page references in *italics* indicate photographs.